# Memories of East Yorkshire

A Collection of Writing
by
Local Authors

Memories from East Yorkshire first edition November 1991.


The publishers would like to dedicate this book to all those Yorkshire people living away from their native East Riding.


Compiled, published and printed by Mason Publications, Driffield, YO25 OHA.
The publishers would like to thank the following, for without their contribution this book would not have been possible.
A. Mason, Rose Hutchinson, R. Howden, Winnie Sellars, A. Waites, H. L. Day, I. Briggs, J. Stephenson, Paul Everatt, G. E. Hume, Bill Thompson, J. W. Stephenson, Mike Wilson, Stanley L. Cooper, Christopher Ketchell and the Local History Archives Unit, Mary Randell, Marilyn White, R. H. Smith, R. N. Lister, Ted Tuxworth, F. Hoggard, F. Rogers, M. A. Danby, Janet Hearn, F. Peeke, Spur Photo's, E. W. Slater.


No part of this book may be reproduced, stored in a retrieval system or transmitted in any form, or any means electronic, mechanical, photocopying, recording or otherwise without the prior permission of the Publishers and the Copyright holders.

ISBN 0 9518832 0 8

# CONTENTS

Chiltern Street Remembered
  By Anne Mason ............................. 5
Leavening — A Wolds Village
  By Rose Hutchinson ......................... 10
Thorganby in 1908
  By R. Howden ............................... 13
My Home in Terry Street
  By Winnie Sellars .......................... 19
My Garton
  By A. Waites ............................... 23
The Cricketing Bishops
  By P. G. Mason ............................. 27
Martinmas Day
  By H. L. Day ............................... 31
Early Tram Days in Hull
  By A. Mason ................................ 36
Old Bridlington Days
  By I. Briggs ............................... 41
Childhood Days in Burton Agnes
  By J. Stephenson ........................... 47
Boyhood Memories of Brough
  By Paul Everatt ............................ 51
Filey — Episodes and Anecdotes
  By G. E. Hume .............................. 53
The Story of a Waggoner
  By Bill Thompson ........................... 59
Chicken Joe and the Shamrocks
  By J. W. Stephenson ........................ 63
A Train Spotter Remembers
  By Mike Wilson ............................. 67
Life in Sproatley in the 30's
  By Stanley L. Cooper ....................... 69

Cover Picture by kind permission of Marilyn White.

# Chiltern Street Remembered
## By Anne Mason

They say as you get older, you tend to drift back into the past more. Now that I am just over the "golden age" I can understand how easy it is to do just that.
When you are young and hear older folk talking about their memories you are inclined to smile, nod and say "Oh yes, fancy that"... you are not really interested, but that is because you are so young and you have not had time to stow away memories in your mind. It's different when you age, and start to go through your own personal filing system, maybe seeing a building, or hearing a certain tune, even remembering a name can spark it off.
I was born and bred in Hull. I left twenty one years ago and each time I visit, my filing system goes into action and memories come flooding back. Chiltern street, number seventy two, a street of little houses, you walked straight into the kitchen from the street. It was the main room where we ate and sat at night, all doing some simple thing until it was time for bed. There was a scullery in the back where the washing and other menial tasks were carried out. Upstairs were two bedrooms, the larger one to the front and a very small one at the back, with a very narrow twisting stair leading to them.
Outside the scullery door was a small yard that had a cold water tap and sink. The outside 'closet' and coalhouse stood side by side. Beyond the yard was a very long garden, and for all this my mum paid the grand sum of 2/6d a week (12½p). But considering my dads wage at that time was only 18/- per week (90p) and no family allowance (child benefit as it now is called) it did not leave much for other things.
I was born in 1925, and can only speak of what I remember after that date. One of my early recollections was attending Chiltern Street school which was just at the bottom of the street. At play time, my sister Eva used to bring me a snack, as my mum was worried in case I was hungry. Being the baby of the family I was always fussed over, anyway, Eva would pass the food through the big iron gates and wait until I had scoffed the lot, then off she would go coming back at lunch time to collect me.
I got a penny a week pocket money and had to do a little job to earn that. But as there were four other girls and two boys, this meant my job was cleaning my dads boots, nothing very hard. The penny I got went a long way, as there were four farthings in a penny and you could spend a farthing at a time. For this you were able to get a big bag of 'goody dust' or two 'gob stoppers' or some damaged fruit. There was no end to the selection you could get from the many shops in the street. Then there was Pennas ice cream, you could get a big cup full of lovely yellow creamy ice cream for a halfpenny. They came round every day, a brightly painted cart pulled by a little fat pony we all made a fuss over.

The entertainers came down the street all the time. After tea we played 'boolers' (rolling a hoop by hitting it with a stick) but that was soon put aside when the singers came along. A man and a woman would walk in the gutter from one end of the street to the other, singing the popular song of the time. They had lovely voices I recall, they had a little girl with them who went round collecting any money she could. Then there was the dancing bear. A man dressed (what I now know) in a Tyrol type suit, short trousers with braces and an embroidered jacket and a funny hat. He would play a concertina and the bear would dance. It was attached to a long chain fastened to a collar around its neck, it looked so sad with its big snout covered by a muzzle. Thank goodness it has been stopped now.

We sat on the kerbs edge many times watching the acrobats and a man on tall stilts. They came round when Hull fair came to the town. A troupe would come round drumming up customers, but we did not think that then, we just enjoyed it so much and watched enthralled. To us they were creatures from another world.

The organ grinder was another big draw. When he came round complete with his little chattering monkey we would all dance in the road we thought it was great. Anything with animals drew us all out. When the Atora suet waggon came down the street we were so excited we knocked on peoples doors telling them to come out and see this new wonder. The waggon was just like you see in cowboy pictures, and was pulled by two of the biggest animals we had ever seen. They were oxon and were so gentle we could touch them, which was wonderful, we followed them to the end of the street and watched them until they disappeared out of view.

In the evening the 'hot pea man' would come round. We would get a basin full of mushy peas and share them in cups, with vinegar on, they were delicious. On a Sunday morning the watercress man would appear, a tray on his head and shouting, "fresh watercress" at the top of his voice.

The gas lighter, a thin faced man with a big curly moustache always had a pipe in his mouth. You could tell when he was around, his tobacco smelt lovely. He would come down the street with a big long pole and on the end there was a brass hook for opening the glass door of the lamp. With the pole he would then switch on the gas and with a plop on would come the light. The door closed and on to the next one. We knew it was time to go in when he appeared.

If you had to be up early for work in the mornings, three or four o clock some people, you could ask the 'knocker up' to give you a call, for sixpence a week (2½p) he or she would come to your window with a large pole and bang on the glass to wake you. You had to show your face before they would go away. This brought a little extra income to the family if this job was taken on.

My mother kept a spotless house. The older girls helped with the house work, for though it was only a small house things were never done by half. We did not have any carpet sweeper, washer or dish washer, nor a fancy cooker, everything was done the hard way.

The big black stove in the kitchen was black leaded every day of the week. All the brass (and the hearth was full of it) was cleaned every week. The boiler at the side was filled with water each time it got low, this had a brass tap on the front so you could fill your bucket or whatever, and you always had hot water. The stove had to be done before my sisters went to

school, and this was not easy with a fire burning. Whoever's turn it was would be sweating buckets whilst brushing away at the stove.

The fireside had a large tin plate that was laid down in front of the fire about three feet long and one foot wide, this was usually decorated with flowers of some kind. On this rested the brass. A big curb went right round the tin plate encasing it, this too was made of heavy brass very ornate, all curls and fancy bits. On the short ends of this rested the irons, these were a pair of tongs, a poker, shovel and rake, the latter was used for pulling the coals forward from the back of the fire. They were all about thirty inches long.

If you were well off you had a pair of 'dogs' on which the irons rested, these too could be quite ornate. Of course a tidy was a must, this kept the ashes in place, this too was made completly of brass. At each side of the tidy backing onto the fire place lay two brass sills to finish it all off.

The mantle shelf was very high, and draped with a heavy shaped cover edged with baubles, usually deep red velvet, which was always removed on wash days to make room for all the clothes which were hung around the fire if it was raining.

Now wash day was a right ritual, mum would be up at cock crow, the little copper in the outhouse was lit and filled with water. All the mats taken up and the scrubbing table brought out of the scullery and put in the yard. This was not the real beginning of wash day. The previous day being Sunday meant all the white were put into soak ready for the next day. Then on Monday they would be ready to be put into the copper and boiled for an hour, scrubbed and then dollied and finally rinsed under the running cold water tap in the yard and blued, ready for the next day to be put through the mangle and hung out. The coloureds came next, and were given an equally thorough treatment. When all the clothes had been disposed of, it was the turn of the clothes basket, basses and anything else that needed a weekly scrub. The yard would be swilled and donkey stoned.

After the clothes were dried they were pulled into shape, folded and piled up ready for ironing. This was done with flat irons which were heated on the fire. Most things were starched, so care had to be taken when ironing them, or else they would crease badly. All this hard work paid off, the clothes were always lovely and white and clean, and at the time only soda and naptha soap was used, no soap powders.

My mum and dad were very strict in those days. No one was allowed to talk at the table during meals or come to the table with dirty hands, and no one left it either until my parents said so. We were all very well looked after. My mum was a wonderful cook and made a big batch of bread twice a week. Big pots of stew and dumplings, my favourite were her oven cakes, we used to dip them in tomatoe gravy (I've never tasted gravy like that since, I can never get it like she did.) Beef dripping with the black at the bottom of the pot, that was a treat indeed, for we could not afford a lot of meat. When I think back, my word she must have been a wonderful manager as not a lot of money came into the house.

The things we played at were so simple, but they kept us occupied for ages, we had fun too having races. Whip and top, boolers, skipping, a big rope stretched across the street and we all joined in chanting the skipping poems, the winner would get a dip in the kalie bag with a wet finger. People came to the door selling things, my dad bought me a desk and stool for 3/6d (17½p) the stool was a bit rickety so my dad made me one, a sturdy little thing that I still have today.

When anything happened in the street everyone would come out of their houses 'to see' "are you coming to see?" we would shout to each other. Anyway this woman had 'turned to sugar' so us kids were told by Alice Grey, she knew everything. For weeks it was the topic and puzzlement of how a woman could turn to sugar, of course now we knew, poor woman had diabetes.

Then Alice Grey told us about a neighbour who was taken away in an ambulance. She said the person had both her eyes out, and we all wondered at the sight of her face with two holes in it. To beat that, Alice Grey knew for certain the baby born at number 46 had been born inside out, and had to be wrapped in cotton wool and bandaged to stop its heart and things falling apart. We were enthralled at this gory tale and gaped in awe at the house each time we passed. I'm sure Alice Grey must have ended up as a writer, writing a most descriptive medical book.

Roundabouts came down the street pulled by a stout horse, and a halfpenny would give you a good long ride. I cant remember seeing the country or seaside until I was much older.

It was an event to have a funeral. Days before, all the curtains would be drawn in every window as a sign of respect. On the day of the funeral we would all gather outside the house and watch wide eyed as the coffin was carried out to the waiting hearse. This was a square glass thing with an ornate top and corners, pulled by two shining black horses adorned with plumes on their heads. A man would walk in front of them, he too was all in black and wore a top hat. I never knew why he was there, but thought it was to show them the way. The mourners completely in black would follow in carriages pulled by one horse. Of course the cost of this was always saved up for, maybe a life time, paid to the insurance man every week to make sure you had a good send off. If you had a bit over you were 'put away with ham' that meant a good ham tea was provided after the funeral. Some folk would attend all the funerals they could, just for the tea, the cost of all this would barely pay for the coffin today.

I had a friend called Becky Harrison who was always off school for some reason or other. When the boardman went round to find out why, her mother would sit at the piano and sing to him "Abie, Abie, Abie my boy" at the top of her voice, and he would give up and go away. His name was Abraham, and he was very embarrassed at the musical outburst everytime he called. There must have been some words in the song that had hidden meanings. I never did find out.

There was a dairy at the top of the street and we could watch the cows been driven in and milked. We bought our milk there. I use to take a jug, my mum would say "dont drink the milk", but I could not resist a sip, it tasted good, it was so creamy. Later on they called at the house with a churn and measured out just what we wanted. So much for hygiene, we never ailed much for all that.

As our family grew we had to move from our little house, 'flitting' as it was called. We moved to a much larger house in Arnold crescent off Arnold street on Anlaby road. It was before the East Yorkshire garages were built, there was a huge house with steps leading up to the front door, and big stone lions at each side, (those lions ended up on the steps of the Criterion cinema down George street, it is'nt there now.

It was easy to get a house then, you just walked around the area you wished to move to and choose the empty house you liked the look of, get the address off the owner from the poster in the window, and go for the key. When you had decided that you liked it you moved in and cleaned it out before putting a stick of furniture in it.

Our new house brought much happiness and pain. As we grew up lots of things happened both to our family and the world. But you can always have your memories cant you?

# Leavening — A Wolds Village

By Rose Hutchinson

Rose Hutchinson 2nd left with mum and Land Army girls.

I remember, I remember the house where I was born,
The little windows where the sun came peeping in at morn.
It never came a wink too soon or brought too long a day.
But now, I often wish the night had borne my breath away.

I was born on May 9th, 1926 at Southfield Farm, Leavening, the eldest of two daughters of George Harold and Ethel May Varey.
The farm house is situated near the cross roads on the York side of the village. The land is to the south between Leavening and Leppington and both sides of the road, once ninety one acres, but now slightly under, around eighty six. Small areas have been bought by the council for sewerage works, cemetery and road widening.
It is now owned by Mrs Ethel Anne Holtby (2nd daughter) and farmed by Robert Holtby, son, this being the 4th generation to run the farm.
Leavening is supposed to have got its name thus: the people were so poor the inhabitants lived mostly on bread. Leaven (flat cake, bread), and Ings (the grasslands besides the river or beck).
There have been many changes in the village over the past century. Several houses have been built, many pulled down or fallen down. At the present day there are 93 dwellings in the village itself. The Methodist schoolroom was built in 1910 on Chapel Hill, and a Council school around the same time up the back lane. A new farm was built just beyond this in 1948, also being a Council property.
The Primitive Chapel has gone, first being sold for use as a barn, then pulled down, before making way for a new ultra modern bungalow with dorma. This is named Ranters Cottage.
Like the buildings, the people have changed too. The present schoolmistress, Mrs Taylor, came to Leavening in 1987 bringing modern teaching methods
I remember well how Mr. Harold Walsh and his wife Florence (1929-54) gave their all to village affairs, taking on many duties, Church Warden, Councillor, Adviser, M.C. at dances (village hops) and whist drives and any other thing they asked him. Also Mr. Tony Haggard and Mr. Jack Pile who followed in his footsteps, though each had different personalities. There was a Mr. Groves who didn't reign long.
Many people now come to the village and don't stay long, do not join in anything and are no asset to the village life as we know it. Forgive this comment, but I am an 'old timer' who also appreciates much of modern day living.

Should the health giving properties of the Yorkshire Wolds require any boosting, the old fashioned village of Leavening offers a tangible illustration, for it is doubtful if any Wolds village of its size possesses such a large number of long lived residents. It has a score of residents well over septuagenarian age. These people will tell you of the days when the journey to Malton or York was a nightmare in a carriers cart.

I well recall the glory of the old club feast. No longer do the youth of the village dance to the tune of a melodium or young men gather at the tailor's or shoemaker's during the winter evenings.

Everything has changed, and these old folks whose reminiscences are recorded tell you of them in plain unvarnished language. One link with the past, however, was the penfold which existed until a few years ago and was utilised for straying cattle.

In 1935 Mrs. Mary Ann Bogg the eldest resident passed her 80th birthday, those were the days she states when everybody kept a pig to kill at Christmas. Her husband was a carrier between the village and York, and experienced many rough journeys they had through snowstorms when they often had to leave the road and go through fields to avoid snowdrifts. In winter he used to set off at three in the morning to get to York at a decent time.

Travellers from the West Riding would visit the famous Stamford Bridge Fair and sell their cloth to the farmers. The tailors would then go to the farmer and make clothes before he left to go to another farm. This practice was known as whipping the cat.

In former days the club feast and Sunday School anniversary were the 'big days' in the village each year, and on the occasion of the latter nearly everyone, Church or Chapel, attended.

Country houses played a great part in the social life of villages. Mr. Mooring refers in affectionate terms to the sterling qualities of the late Major-General Northcliffe of Langton, a good landlord who studied his tenants' interests at Christmas time, providing them with half a ton of coal, a piece of beef and sixpence.

Mr. John Carr, known as 'Witty' because of his ready wit, was still following his occupation as a mole catcher at the age of seventy-six. A quaint character, 'Witty' always has a ready answer. His family have been mole catchers for two hundred years. He also played the melodium for the youths and maidens to dance to.

During the 1939-45 war the bus never stopped running. Many's the times it carried two or three times the number it was supposed to do. We were packed like herrings in a box and Herbert Peterkin hardly ever failed to drive her home. Sometimes it had to be abandoned in the snow. Herbert died in the bus one Saturday night after dropping off his last passenger at the crossroads.

Edgar Milner was the cycling postman. He was one of the strong men in his day and at one time had the Hare and Hounds pub plus a little cycle shop. We all went to him for assistance at sometime. He had his own brand of cycle, the 'Wold Ranger', which he built and sold for the princely sum of ten guineas.

He use to sort the letters out between the keys on his piano. This was not regulation orders. He would then set off on his bike to deliver them.

There is no longer Mrs Varey's tea-room on the crossroads.

This was a lifetime ago, where all passers-bye were welcomed and I spent my Sundays washing up.

Electricity was brought to the village in the mid fifties. We are also on a new water supply, no longer using the lovely spring water of which there is ample, all in the name of progress. Before water was piped to the area and we used the local supply, there was no charge: now water rates are high.

There was a strong Home Guard of between 30-40 men under the command of Lieutenant Sagar of Malton and J.H. Peterkin (Sergeant) They regularly attended parades and lectures. Many specialised in various branches of infantry work and there were some fine marksmen.

Leavening was a reception area for evacuees and about two hundred people at various times found homes in the village. The school admitted 135 children, at one time outnumbering the local children.

Quite a number of Land Girls came to work in the area. Some stayed and married farmers sons. They had some tough jobs to do, especially those who worked with the threshing machine. Most were girls who had never been on a farm before, but they did a marvellous job and proved their worth.

On December 9th, 1943, a Halifax bomber crashed, narrowly missing houses on the brow side of the village. Two crew members baled out, but five others perished in the blaze.

During the harvest of 1945 (I think it was) Robert Dent, who farmed Boudales Farm at the time, went to straighten a stook of corn in the field and was blown up and severely injured by a bomb of some kind that had laid in the field, possibly for a while.

A piece of land was bought from Mr. Varey by the council and a cemetery was consecrated. It lies on the road to Leppington a good half mile from the village. The funny thing about this is the church people are buried at one end and the Chapel people at the other. Heaven knows what will happen when they meet in the middle.

An helping hand.

# Thorganby in 1908

By R. Howden

Thorganby is situated on the western side of the River Derwent; to the north lies Wheldrake and to the south North Duffield.
The village of West Cottingwith is now incorporated with the village of Thorganby. The church stands between the two villages. At that time there were two services, one in the morning and one in the evening.
Thorganby Hall is opposite the church and the Methodist Chapel which, built in 1909, is in the village in a very convenient position.
Many preachers had to walk whilst others cycled. Some had horses and traps. The farmers provided food and shelter for the horse.
Near the chapel stood the general store, which supplied most of the items needed for the daily routine of life. The shop window was at the south end of the property and the entrance was close by.
Further along the main road was the joiner's shop. This property was a continuation of houses. The property stood end to the road. It was the custom in those days to make up your own paint from powder and red and white lead.
Unlike the Joiner's shop, the Blacksmith's shop had a good road frontage which provided accommodation for implements awaiting repair. This frontage also provided a space for the 'hooping ring'. (the large metal tyre that ran on the outside of wooden cart wheels). Hooping was carried out quite frequently and extra help was needed. The hoops were heated by forming a circle with segments, which could be made to the size required. These segments were so designed to hold the fire needed. The wheel was placed on the hooping ring which had a centre large bolt, which went through the centre of the wheel and a block of wood across and then an iron plate on top of the wood and a large screw device was turned onto the centre bolt and tightened up. This made the wheel very firm. The heated hoop was lifted as required and placed on the wheel. I can still see the flames and smoke coming from around the rim of the wheel. A barrel of water was at hand as soon as the hoop had been forced down to the hooping ring by hammer. It was a case of rushing to put water on the hot hoop. As the hoop contracted you could hear the wheel joints being brought closer together.
The Blacksmith's was run by my father and brother with one apprentice, and later a cycle business was added. Cycles were only just becoming available. To the ordinary working folk of the day it was no mean effort to save up for a cycle as wages were very low, and the condition of the roads were no

encouragement. With the advent of the cycle came the usual accessories: bag of spanners, cycle clips, lamps and carbide for the acetylene lamps. The oil lamp had a special oil, very refined for the purpose. Rear lamps were not required at that time; it was not until around 1914-18 that rear lights were introduced. There were also candle lamps used as a cycle light, of which I had one.

We had two well known characters who visited the village. One was Bill Rowley the travelling chimney sweep with a top hat. He always made his home on the hearth of the blacksmiths shop. He would cook bacon and egg on the dying embers of the forge fire. It was impossible to see his mouth; his face was a mass of whiskers. He would sometimes stay a few days depending on the weather. The shop door was never locked when Billy was around. He was very honest and accepted as part of the rural way of life.

Snowden Slieghts, a well known wild fowler, was the other character to visit the village. He would call to have lunch over the warm forge fire. We would watch him manouevre his boat, shaped like a floating log. He used trees as a cover, and when the ducks were within range he would fire his large gun. He had a dog with him and immediately the gun was fired it would jump out of the boat and retrieve the birds. There were many birds on the flood waters at the time.

On August 1st, 1848, the Selby/Market Weighton railway was opened. Before this, all goods in or out of the village were conveyed by boat. Even when the railway at Cliff Common (DVLR) opened there would still have been a considerable amount of carting.

When the railway came it was much easier to transport belongings. One lad leaving the farm at Martinmus to go home carried his box from Common Farm along by West Grange, over the fields to Skipwith Common and along the road to Cliff Common station, six mile in all. I think he would have been pleased when he got there.

Martinmus Monday was the day when the farmers and workers, including the married women, made their way to Selby market. The farmers stood near the Abbey, whilst the lads and lasses stood at the other end of the market near the Banks. Usually most of them, farmers and workers, found someone suitable to both sides before the day was finished. After the market and the hiring the rest of the evening was spent at the fair held in Wide street.

Another highlight of our school days was the village agricultural show. This was held on the Friday and Saturday of the August Bank holiday week-end, later to become a one day event, on the Barn field near the buildings of Thorganby Hall Farm. The stock was tied to the railings along the ings side of the field and the show ring was central, to the advantage of those preparing their stock.

There was always good produce on display in the horticultural tent which also included agricultural produce and entries of various handy work, childrens wild flowers etc. Little did I think as I went around the tents as a child with my parents that I would in later life judge the horticultural exhibits. I judged at many shows around East Yorkshire, yet I found no better produce than at Thorganby show.

A very smart horse drawn waggon would bring the band that was in attendance throughout the period of the show.

The day before the show any lads coming from West Cottingwith would bring the news of any fair people who had arrived. The

Bill Rowley the travelling chimney sweep.

roundabouts were the main attraction. I remember when riding round, one could hear the hiss of steam as you passed the organ. The steam and the oil together provided a smell that one does not readily forget, and many times in my life I have come across oil and steam together which never failed to bring back memories.

The lighting for the amusements was provided by pear shaped lamps hung from the stalls. They had a long stem from the container to the burner, very much like a small gas ring with long bright flames. They even managed to stay alight in strong winds, swinging backwards and forwards.

There was something about the village feast that will always bring back memories for those who were able to partake in the events. One could hear the steam organ and the laughter of young people echoing through the village until a late hour.

The only means of transport before the railway was by carrier, horse and trap or cycle. The local carrier, usually two horses and a four wheeled cart, made the journey to Selby on Mondays and York on Saturdays. Relatives who came to visit in those days stayed for a week at least, arriving at York or Selby by train, thence by carrier to the villages.

I should mention here that poultry and produce was put on the pavement at Selby, outside the Midland Bank. I have seen the pavement crowded with buyers, sellers and produce. Hens would sell for four shillings a pair (20p). Eggs sold for a shilling a dozen but prices varied according to season, in winter they were very scarce. Deep litter and battery cages were unknown in those days.

We suffered very severe winters, which in turn made the ings a sea of ice. Nearly every house in the village had a pair or pairs of skates. The ladies had wooden ones whilst the men

Thorganby Agricultural Show 1908.

Rail Car on the Derwent Valley Railway.

had much heavier metal ones. All were fastened to the boots by a screw attachment Most of the younger generation took advantage of the facility to skate. Those who could not skate or who had no skates were brought onto the ice and pushed around in chairs.

News became more available, because the DVLR had arrived. It made it possible to have an evening newspaper, which gave information about the development of the war (1914-18). In the school was a large map, and flags of all nations was supplied to pin on the map. Also in nearly every house the same map and pins were supplied.

Air raid warnings were sent to West Cottingwith and someone came around with the information.

I was standing on the north side of the chapel with my sister and we heard a droning sound coming from the east. As it got nearer and overhead we saw the zeppelin, which looked like a large cigar in the sky. It made off in the direction of Eskrick and then turned towards York and bombs were dropped on the city.

Whilst on the subject of airships, we were not many miles away from Howden Airship station and it was not an uncommon sight to see airships around when the weather was suitable.

I note in my diary of Thursday, February 14th, 1917, I have an entry which gives the information that I saw four airships, a Fish and 2 Cubords, 2 basket ones, (these would be large ones. R100 class) and a blue pig. These were names we gave to various types of airship and has no resemblance.

Also during the war we saw our first aeroplane, it came down behind the church which was grass land.

I left school in 1914; I was thirteen years old. At that time many of the young men were called up into the forces; this in turn created a shortage of farm labour. Wages were very low: a man would earn about 90p per week for a nine hour day six days a week, and how the workers brought up large families as they did, always remained a mystery to me. Most cottages had two pigs each a year. Both were fattened up for around Christmas time. One would be killed for own use and the other sold to buy necessities, such as clothes and boots. The main stay for a hot meal was the meat and potatoe pie, followed by apple pie and a pot of tea.

On some of the large wold farms in the kitchen stood a large table with a solid wooden top. Along the sides hollows were cut out the size of a dinner plate and fairly deep, also at both ends one was cut out. The foreman had to sit at one end and the youngest lad at the other. Broth was then poured in at the foreman's end and ran via a channel to each of the other places. The table was level and by the time each place was full, it was back to the foreman who gave the order to commence eating. The main meal was also placed in the hollows and after that a large piece of pie was placed on the table with a pint of hot tea. The maid then had to scrub down the table after each meal.

Many young folk will not understand what life was like. It was life in the full, the smell of the hay and may blossom. The roads were not full of motor cars. The stillness at night that could be felt.

This was my life and I enjoyed every minute to the full, and now it fills me with admiration that I had been born into an environment of this kind.

A day out to Bridlington.

# My Home in Terry Street
By Winnie Sellars

Terry Street isn't there anymore - well, not the Terry Street I knew. I loved living down there from the first moment we moved in. From the early forties to the early fifties this was home.

There were a couple of terraces and a beer-off shop on one side. The beer-off sold all sorts, bread, trays of buns on the wooden counter, and the shelves behind were lined with patent medicines, sweets and cigs. It was a real treasure trove.

We lived in a front house on the other side of the street. I was glad about that, as we always seemed to catch more sun. It's funny about houses, some are just that - houses, others welcome you, make you feel you belong. Number forty-two was one of those, and as soon as I walked in I felt at home. We stepped in straight from the pavement, over the wide yellow step. Dad painted it that colour, to save mum the eternal job of using the donkey-stone every day. All that was needed was a quick wash over, including a couple of flagstones around the doorway (everyone did it), and it was as smart as anyone else's down the street.

Appearances were important, and the brown front door and wide windowledge of the front room also had to be spic and span. The front door led into a long narrow passage, with the front and middle room doors on the left. The front room was sacred, only for 'best'. I'm not sure what 'best' was supposed to be, but it didn't come around very often, as the room was rarely used. The new three-piece suite in flowered brocade dominated the room. I say 'new', because no-one hardly ever sat on it, and the beige cotton chair covers remained uncreased from one wash-day to the next.

The only other big piece of furniture was a lovely dark wood piano. Its keys gleamed startling white, and for several years until I 'took up' the piano briefly for six months, it also remained untouched, except for its weekly dust.

Dusting was my job in there. Mam would say, "School's over for the week!" and she'd put a duster in my hands and tell me to "try and frame" every Saturday morning. She usually added that remark, as being left-handed I was in need of extra instructions she believed. I enjoyed lifting the ornaments, studying the details, and carefully putting them back in exactly the same place. That was essential.

The blue and white china old-fashioned couple needed extra care; the lady's head had somehow become detached, and was held in place by a long matchstick. This joined the hollow in her head to the hollow in her neck, and I sometimes left her facing the wrong way to give her a change of view.

The china castle on the mantlepiece need great care too, and woe betide me when I 'forgot' to dust the empty fireplace. "What if somebody came in, whatever would they think?" Mam was scandalised. I dont know why, no-one ever did go in the room much, it was far too cold. Probably because the fire was never lit, though it was laid ready 'just in case'. Visitors, expected or otherwise, tramped straight down the passage to the kitchen at the end. We lived there. The passage veered to the left at the foot of the stairs, past the middle room door, (this room was also rarely used) to the hub of the house. We'd pause long enough to hang our outdoor things on the high curly hooks, then rush into the kitchen. On the right was a black Yorkist range, flanked by huge green-painted cupboards on either side. One for ironing, the other for oddments. Oddments could be anything from a biscuit tin to a recently demised budgie's cage.

The fire in the grate was not very often out; even at night it was heaped with coal-slack to keep the place 'aired'. The huge kettle, blackened with soot at the back, always waited on the hob. When someone appeared in the doorway, the kettle was firmly embedded in the flames, and the teapot put to warm.

Piles of neatly chopped firewood lay in bundles at one side of the hearth, and a large metal bucket of mixed coal and cinders stood 'at the ready', on the other side. Two black collie dogs flanked the fireside, while close by were two relics of the Great War. One was the black painted case of a Mills bomb, and the other an enormous highly polished bullet shellcase. These two, along with a small fancy clog which rested in the place of honour on the mantlepiece, and bore the name Zeebrugge in burnt poker work, had come down to us from a distant relative. They were greatly treasured by us all.

Beverley Road Colliseum and Palladium staff Christmas 1913

The huge wooden table in the bay opposite the fireplace was never without its covering of oilcloth, except for its ritual scrub. Beautiful purple grapes and exotic red and yellow fruits filled everyone of the oilcloth's many squares.
Scones or fruit pies kept on the oven top were usually handed round when tea was poured.
Two ancient, but comfortable, armchairs stood at each end of the multi-coloured 'rag' rug, and Tiddles our plain but loveable Tabby cat was never far away.
We didn't know how old Tiddles was; Dad had found her in the ruins of a bombed house, hiding in the bottom of a broken chest of drawers. He brought her home, covered in dust, and she took to us immediately. It wasn't often she ventured out of sight.
The kitchen opened onto a small verandah with indoor coalhouse and bathroom. The bathroom had been intended as a pantry, but a previous tenant had done a rough conversion of his own. Even so, we were grateful for his efforts, although we could only use a few inches of water for the bath. It was much appreciated.
Our pride and joy was the backway. A little concrete yard led onto a tiny garden with its pocket-size square of grass. Dad grew marigolds and an occasional assortment of annuals, sweet peas or virginia stock, etc.
From somewhere or other he acquired an old garden seat which he installed at the bottom of the garden. On fine days, he would come home from work, take a pint mug of strong tea (sweetened with condensed milk) out there, and sit in the sun while his tea was ready.
In the corner, near the fence, he had a patch of rhubarb, and one year when it looked particularly fine he said, "I'll leave it a bit longer, it'll be all the better", and he covered it with a bucket to force it. Dad's face was a picture a day or two later, when I helped him 'unveil' it. Every stick had gone - somebody unknown had already decided the rhubarb was ready for eating. A narrow cinder track ran past the end of the gardens, alongside the railway line, so the culprit could have been anyone.
The trains going past at regular intervals did not bother us at all; in fact the sound of the wagons being shunted in the darkness of the night was quite a comfort at times. The railway station was just around the corner of Beverley road, and after the war we had a few trips to Withernsea. These were great fun, and I remember the excitement of waiting on the platform among the crowds waiting for the train to come in. We'd rush through the clouds of steam and try for a carriage with empty corner seats; these were best to watch the landscape coming or going through the flying smoke. The squeal of brakes and the slamming of doors at every small station along the way added to the drama. The favourite sight was that of the lighthouse appearing on the horizon in the far distance. I enjoyed the journey better than the actual day out, and the highlight was when the train was turned round on the track at the end of the line. Railwaymen armed with iron levers operated the huge turntable in front of an army of interested passengers, ready for the journey home.
Occasionally we went to the pictures. There wasn't far to go as the National was only at the bottom of the street. Second house was thought to be best, and we'd walk there about a quarter to eight, and join the queue. There was always a queue, and it often wound out the front of the National and right down the side, if the film was a good one. The excitement was felt

when we began to move nearer to the ticket office. The manager in his smart suit with white shirt and bow tie stood close to the window, just moving now and again to inform those at the front there were "three doubles" or "two singles" in the middle, and "move along - if you please!" The relief was enormous when we were finally installed while the interval lights were still on, and we could be comfortably settled before the 'Pathe News Gazette'. Afterwards I would go to bed, up the steep stairs, and holding on to the polished bannister to turn at the top. Three more steps and into my room. It seemed quite big, with acres of cold lino under my feet, but I didn't envy the others except for one thing. In one of the other bedrooms was my favourite picture. A country scene of a field with some trees, and a few sheep grazing. Underneath the picture were a few lines, something like this, "No time to stand beneath the boughs, and stare around like sheep and cows." I always felt that was very special.

Yes, for about ten years at school, then work, Terry street was home. And however good a day or night out had been, I was always glad to be back there.

Mrs Sellars father in the garden
of their home in Terry Street

# My Garton
## By A. Waites

Of all the places in this wide world of ours, which I have been fortunate to visit, none of them gave the thrill and pleasure, or the longing to return to them, as did my home village of Garton on the Wolds.

I wasn't actually born there, but at the age of three or four I became a member of its community, and, ofcourse, at five years of age I went to its tiny school. I was taught as an infant by Miss Kitty Appleyard, and then as I progressed into the senior classes, it was old Mr John Stainer who took me in charge, and there I remained until the ripe old age of fourteen. Then it was off to work on the farm.

My home through all those school years was the lovely old cottage at Church farm where, throughout my childhood days, with my five sisters and three brothers, I lived a happy carefree life. The old village church stood only a matter of a hundred yards from my home, and to this day it still gives me a thrill when I see its towering figure shimmering in the sunlight as I drive along the old station road, approaching the village.

A lot of the names of the people who dwelt in Garton are still remembered by me, such as: Frank Dee who was the farmer at West End farm. Billy Monkman and Mr Dale Robinson who also was a farmer at the Cedar House farm.

I remember too the old public house, then built of blocks of chalk. Its name then was the Green Tree. The Kay family with their little farm, followed by the blacksmiths shop, where Mr William Cooper use to shoe the horses, and then the little sweet shop run by Mrs Robinson. Lance Boyes the butcher was next, where many a day I have had to go and fetch six pennyworth of liver and suet.

Across the road from the butcher's was old Art Wilson with his threshing set. But the next farm was, to me, the best kept and tidiest in the village. Old George Robinson was the farmer at Crufts farm, and at harvest time his stacks of corn by the roadside were always 'theaked' to perfection, a real joy to the eyes of any great countryman.

Marson's shop came next and then, ofcourse, we had to have a village joiner, and this duty was performed by Mr Jackson, together with his two sons, Ralph and John.

The biggest farm in the village, opposite the 'mar' (village pond) was the farm of Mr W.B.Atkinson, who also owned Church farm where I lived, and my dad worked as a shepherd for over forty years. It was where I too started my working life. The name of this huge estate was Manor farm. Close beside the gate leading up to the farm was a little cottage. This was the village post office, looked after by Mrs Jessie Butler, with her very lanky son, Alfred, who used to deliver the mail to outlying farms, ploughing his way across the fields, and down many leafy lanes. He was a very good servant to the community.

Just past the post office was the Wesleyan chapel, and then you came to what we use to call 'bottom end', on past the houses of Fred Wilson and the Armstrongs. Across the road was a row of little cottages (no longer there now) and in them lived the Covills, Johnstones and poor old George Banks. he was a rum character, who would walk the three miles to Driffield nearly every day to put his bets on his fancied horses.

Then we come to the Primitive chapel, followed by the small holding run by the Coverdales, who always had plenty of old cows and these, along with other small holder's herds, would be taken altogether by one man, who would proceed to various places, such as Station road, and there the cows devoured the grass at the side of the road, keeping it all neat and trim. Who the cow tender was I cannot recall.

Another row of cottages which housed old Mrs Waines and the Masseys came next. Ernest Massey was my greatest school pal, and even to this day we still keep in touch, although he is now a cripple and lives in Cornwall.

Mrs Gertie Wray had her sweets and household necessities shop next. I can always remember the smell of camphor balls, paraffin, aniseed balls and candles, not unpleasant by any means.

A bit further down, near the end of the street, was a little cottage, and above the door was the sign which read, 'George Smith. Tailor.' I dont know why but he always went under the name of 'Shaggy Smith.' His cottage has a special place in my heart for, when my dad finally retired, he and mam bought the old place, and lived therein until they departed this life, and now my unmarried brother Roy still lives there.

So we are nearly out of the village, but across the road, in fact the very last house, became the Wayside Inn, owned and run most efficiently by Mrs Teasdale and her neice Rachel.

Down Street, Garton on the Wolds.

*Pond View, Garton on the Wolds.*

Going out of the village and up 'Parsons Hill' you come to the vicarage, and over the other side to David Pilmore's farm. Now alongside these two places the green lane ran, right to Cottam Bottom or, if you went t'other way, it led you down over the Malton Dodger Railway, and round back over the Garton station crossing and so on up Station road back to the village. That use to be a very favourite walk for all us youths after the church service on a Sunday night. Sometimes, though, we would go t'other way, down to bottom end, up 'Parson Hill' and go straight on until we came to Elmswell corner. There is no corner now, the road has been straightened out, but when I was a lad a nasty old corner was there, and many accidents happened. When we went to play there on Sunday nights, we would be joined by the children of Elmswell, namely Madge and Nellie Thurlow and Tom and Winnie Dixon. We played there until it was time to go home, and then we would leave the place, for at midnight, so we were told, a ghost took over and roamed the area.

Now the people I have mentioned, and many more I haven't, were to me, in my young days, kindly and understanding and, although none of the families were well off, no one ever went hungry or cold, for each one helped the other out in times of difficulty.

Where the houses of Church View now stand used to be one of our favourite areas for using our four wheeled carts. It was then called the hay field. The orchard too, which was adjacent, has also been devoured by the housing programme. But I am thrilled and thankful indeed to say that my old home at Church farm is still standing, and is now occupied by someone who cares, for they have turned it into a museum. I'm so happy that it is still there as a shrine and a monument of all the happy years I spent there in its warm interior.

Garton Village - White building in foreground is now the Venture Inn

Old George Robinson's stackyard is no longer there. Instead of his huge corn stacks, so perfectly made, there is now a row of new houses, all very nice maybe, but in my mind's eye I still prefer to remember the yard as it used to be. It was only corn, but to me it was food for the masses given by the good Lord.

All through my life I have loved dear old Garton, and remember with pride some of my school pals such as; Ernest and Jack Massey, Charlie Fisher, Reg Armstrong, Fred Pilmore, George Dawson, Percy and Stan Cooper and, of course, Shelley Skelton, who was such a crack shot with a catapult. Sadly he left this world last year, and now, after a life of travel and war, and having seen nearly all the seven wonders of the world, nothing gives me greater pleasure than to sit down in my chair and day dream of Garton, of how it used to be. I can still see my dear old dad amongst his beloved sheep, which he tended with such care, until the time came for him to leave them. Now I myself have passed my three score years and ten, and yet I still think of Garton as the best place in the world. No doubt the people who live there now are as kind and considerate as those in my early days. I do hope so, and I hope with all my heart that they too come to love and cherish that little village of my dreams.

# The Cricketing Bishops

By P. G. Mason

Bishop Wilton sits snugly at the foot of the Wolds close to Garrowby hill. Not the sort of place, one would think, where battle would commence. But it was here in 1927 that a bold challenge was thrown down to the rest of the country, that Bishop Wilton could field a cricket team of veteran cricketers all having seventy summers beneath their belts, a necessary qualification to play in the team. They would play any other team whose aggregate ages did not fall below 850 years, and the village did not exceed 1000 inhabitants. Confident that this challenge would never be taken up, these old men of the green sat back on their laurels, but the West Riding village of Sheepridge, near Huddersfield, on hearing that the gauntlet had been thrown down, looked about them. Never being ones to refuse a challenge, they decided that they too could field a team of veterans, so the journey into foreign parts was duly arranged.

The great event was to take place on the afternoon of Wednesday, July 27th, at Bishop Wilton, but the week previous to the match the home side lost one of its key players through the death of the Reverend G.H.Stocks. However, the game was not lacking in spiritual guidance as the Captain of the Sheepridge side was Canon C, Whorlow.

Both teams, in the run up to the great match, had been practising very hard. The Bishop Wilton team had, in fact, scored sixteen runs against a much younger side, whose ages averaged between forty to fifty. They then went on to dismiss their opponents for eleven.

Flushed with victory, the 'Bishops' entered the field as warm favourites to win the match. Not what one would have called a test wicket, the pitch was typical of a rural cricket field, set in a hollow and surrounded by verdant grass of the Wolds pasture.

The West Riding team rolled up in their char-a-banc with lots of enthusiasm, optimism and confidence, together with pouring rain. They pulled up at 'The Fleece Inn', no doubt for liquid refreshment to sustain them through the gruelling time ahead.

Shortly after three o clock the rain ceased, and many spectators arrived from far and wide to view this extraordinary spectacle. Had the weather been better, possibly visitors from more far flung places would have made the journey. However, under leaden skies many strange faces to the area appeared, and with a crowd of over six hundred the players plodded onto the field. It took them a further thirty minutes to decide whether the match should go ahead.

Bishop Wilton cricket team. Wadsworth, Foster, Ware, Anderson, Fountain, Slater, Johnson.

Rain fell at intervals throughout the afternoon, but this did nothing to decrease the enthusiasm of the players or spectators. The match finally got underway at a quarter to four, and little respect was shown for the age of those playing, with gibes being shouted at both teams as the match progressed.
Not only was this an unusual, if not unique, cricket match, the method of scoring runs too, was strange, to say the least. After a short time it was decided running was a bit too much for these elderly gentlemen, so a system of scoring was devised. A series of boundaries were set up, and if the ball was hit past these boundaries, then a run or runs were scored. They may not have been too apt at running, but they could certainly clout the ball. At one time, when play became a bit slow, the spectators began chanting to quicken up the game, so D.F.Dodds for Sheepridge swiped the ball and scattered the crowd.
At the end of the match Sheepridge took the game by thirty-one runs, beating the Bishops by scoring a total of 106 against the home teams 75.
Bishop Wilton then entertained their visitors to tea, where the host, Sandland, the Hon. Secretary, had provided a meal at his home. Canon Whorlow thanked his host and the team for a good match and he looked forward to the return match to be played on the Fartown County ground at Huddersfield.
The match arranged, 'The Bishops', meeting up at 'The Fleece', left home around ten a.m. to a rousing send off. There were three char-a-bancs to accommodate the team and supporters. The fairer sex, not to be out done, were also in attendance, with lots of tips and advice, not to mention chewing gum and sweets. One young damsel even sat on Jimmy Johnson's knee all the way to the ground.
With food and drink aboard, a message was relayed to Huddersfield, to inform them they were on their way. The charas moved off amid a roar of cheers from the locals who had gathered to send them on their way.
As they motored along through York, the passengers were reminded by posters that today was in fact Ebor day, a day when much money would change hands. The traffic was indeed heavy in the opposite direction, as they approached Tadcaster, and it was here where they made their first stop. "This is where they brew the beer" remarked Harry Here, one of the Umpires.
The party made a short visit to the Tower Breweries and were shown round by the head brewer, Mr Northover.
On reaching the outskirts of Sheepridge, people were at their doors waving and shouting all the way to the ground. A finer reception could not have been better had it been royalty visiting the area.
On entering the ground the cheers grew even louder, with the crowd chanting "Where's Job?" and "Good old Job," Captain Job's fame had indeed preceded him. In fact, certain members of the team were concerned in case Job wore himself out before the game, acknowledging everyone.
The two captains inspected the wicket, pegs were placed at intervals as markers for runs, and the sporting Cannon Whorlow led his team out onto the field and awaited the arrival of the 'Bishops' opening pair, Jimmy Johnson and Schoolmaster Bramley.
Four wickets later, for just twelve runs, things certainly looked bad for the 'Bishops' until Quarton Adamson joined Captain Job, and sustained a steady partnership for over an hour. Although rain fell and the umbrellas came out, the teams

continued with Sheepridge frequently changing bowlers in an effort to dislodge the pair.

To the great amazement of the crowd, Job complained of being thirsty, so he called for a drink. The drink came too late for he was bowled for twenty and met his drink at the pavilion steps. After the dismissal of Job the remaining wickets soon fell and they were all out for seventy five, ironically the same score as their last match.

Sheepridge opened their innings with eighty year old Bullock, and Smith who tipped the scales at eighteen stones. Bullock returned to the pavilion after just three bowls and a score of one. Dodds managed four until he too made the journey back, both players at the hands of Job.

Sheepridge took the match once more with ninety five runs. The teams enjoyed a splendid meal in the pavilion after the game with a speech from Cannon Whorlow on what a great event it had been and friendships that had been struck up between the two villages. Amid many handshakes and cheering the 'Bishops' made the return journey and arrived home at eleven o clock.

Sadly that year the 'Veteran Ashes' rested in the shade of the Pennines, with Job Johnson promising that they would be back to nestle in the Wolds the following year.

From what I can gather, there was never another match played.

Many of the players had never been out of the village, and after all the excitement they needed a few days in bed to recover.

# Martinmas Day

By H. L. Day

The method of hiring farm workers for a year as practised by farmers in the past may be considered today as degrading. Yet in the hungry 1920's there were unemployed industrial workers who would have accepted a guaranteed years work and their board regardless. They had no chance, there were too many countrymen out of work. Martinmas Day, 23rd, November was a red letter day in the lives of the hired workers. It was their pay day of the year and they could leave the farm, their place of employment for good. On the other hand they could also be given the opportunity to re-engage for another year.
November was a relaxed period, harvest and wheat sowing had been completed and roots lifted. Ploughing was the order of the day and this caused little anxiety. Hired lads began to count the days to Martinmas. When the great day arrived, instead of ploughing, they were ordered to fill every available space in the building with straw and fill the turnip house. This was for the benefit of the skeleton staff at work during Martinmas week. When this work was completed, the horses were fed, groomed and bedded with straw. This was to be the last time for the men who did not intend to return and there was regret at leaving horses they had worked and cared for.
During Martinmas week in every country town a day was arranged for hirings to take place, usually on the recognised market day. On such an occasion the town was full of country folk. Farmers, foremen and their wives, single workers and also tradesmen from the surrounding villages.
Previous to 1920 there were no bus services in operation and in most areas no convenient railway. A long walk was involved for many of the villagers attending the hirings and it was one of the rare occasions they visited their local town. Relatives and friends met who had not seen each other since the previous Martinmas. They congregated in the Market place to exchange news and this was one of the most pleasant aspects experienced on a hirings day. It was one of the busiest days of the year for the shopkeepers. clothes and boots were bought for the year ahead. Also watches and pocket knives. Hired horsemen were always interested in the brasses on display in the saddler's shop window.
Bargaining took place between master and man regarding a years wage. When agreement was reached, the worker received a 'fist' a small sum of money to seal the bargain. When a lad had completed his first year and received his wage he became independent of his family. After he had paid for his new rig-out he had little left for pocket money, yet he contrived to make this last until Martinmas came round again. In those days independence was a noticeable characteristic of country folk, they considered accepting charity as being degrading.

After the business of hiring and shopping, all the fun of the fair could be enjoyed. Sites had been found in the town to erect stalls, swings and a steam roundabout. In an era when farm men worked long hours and pleasures were few, it was a day to remember and discuss during the dark winter months ahead.

At the hiring fair held at Malton in 1919 a farmer engaged me to be his second horseman. His farm, Millington Grange, was situated above Pocklington and was forty miles from my home. The horses were kept in the stable during the winter months and I knew I would not be able to return home until April when they were turned out to feed and sleep in a pasture. In previous years, I had been able to return from my place to collect my clean laundry and listen to my grandfather reminiscing about his farming experiences in the 19th century.

On the 2nd December of that year the local carrier conveyed my box which contained all my wordly possessions except those I stood up in to Malton station. My grandfather had used this box for the same purpose when he had been a hired worker before 1860.

The next morning I travelled the same road riding my bike to Malton station, on arrival I collected my box from the left luggage office and waited on the appropriate platform for the Scarborough to York express. When it arrived I placed my box and bike in the guards van and then found a seat in a compartment.

In those days identification of a farm horseman was never difficult. The evidence was the colour in their weather-beaten faces and the clothes they wore. I was wearing my working suit made from corduroy and a pair of hob-nailed boots, plus a pair of fustian leggings.

Soon after the train left Malton, a man sitting next to me enquired "Where is the farm you are bound for this year?" After my reply, he said "I am a vet and live at Pocklington and I visit this farm you are going to when my services are required, and hired lads give it a good name." reassuring words. Just before we arrived at York, he informed me that there was only a minute to exchange trains. His help in carrying my box enabled me to push my bike at the same time, otherwise I would have missed my connection. There were so many platforms, finding the right one I needed would have been a problem. On arrival at Pocklington I was given permission to leave my box in the porters room until I came down with a waggon and collected it. Strange as it may seem today, no charge was made.

My journey to the farm was far from easy, and at one stage I had to push my bike up a long hill. Eventually, I arrived, a stranger in a strange farm. The home comforts I had enjoyed were behind me and Martinmas Day was too far away to contemplate.

The hired farm workers' annual holiday was referred to as Martinmas Week, yet it was usually the 3rd of December when they arrived at their places, a period of 10 days. After the comforts of home, I required at least a week to settle, longer if I was a stranger to the farm.

At the hirings I had acquired, through the grapevine, certain information regarding the conditions I should experience. This did not include the horses' names, ages, and habits they may have developed, or the lay of the land. I had to obtain this information from the foreman or a lad who had returned for another year.

In the mid 1920's I was the waggonner at Gleab Farm on the Wolds and Jib Babes was my lad. It comprised 500 acres and during the winter the horses were kept in the stable. It was a recognised condition of employment that six horses should be the limit a man and a lad should be required to look after. There were three stables and in each one there were stalls for six horses. I was in charge of number one stable, third lad number two and fourth lad number three. The dialect names of these were 'Thoddy' and 'Fowatty'. They were so called because they were third and fourth in order of authority - the foreman being the first and myself second. When ploughing was in progress, I was in the lead followed by 'Thoddy', then 'Fowatty' and their respective lads. We looked upon the foreman as the boss and addressed him as such. His responsibility including organising the labour force, culti-vating, sowing and harvesting the crops. If the work was completed in season the master rarely interfered with his plans.

The routine we practised in the stable was universal on all the big Wold farms. At 5am we were out of bed, soon dressed and on our way to the stable.

When I opened the door, there was bedlam. Horses whinnied, kicked the wooden partitions, or stamped. These sounds were music to my ears because hungry horses were in good fettle. The noise soon subsided after I had given each one a feed, a portion of oats and one of chaff. This mixture was contained in a small sieve which enabled me to remove any dust among it before tipping it into the horse's crib. Meanwhile, Jim had made a start to 'muck out' and I joined him. When this work was completed, each horse in turn was allowed a drink out of a trough in the fold yard. When one had returned to its stall it found a second feed in its crib.

I continued to feed the horses and the number of feeds each one received depended on its appetite. I also groomed and harnessed my pair. Jim attended to the remainder likewise, except feeding them.

At 6.30am the foreman on his rounds called at each stable and left orders. I was allowed to select the horses for the work

Mr H. L. Day with his team.

in hand, likewise 'Thoddy' and 'Fowatty'. After I had given the horses their last feed, we wended our way to the house where breakfast was served.

We imagined we owned the tools and ploughs we used and the horses we were allocated. The word 'my' often crept into our conversation on and off the farm. This imaginary ownership was most evident when we were at work in the stable for we never used each other's cutty-comb, dandy-brush or muck fork. A lads tools were always second best. Should his dandy-brush wear out, the horseman in charge claimed the new replacement. We were each allocated a wagon and mine was kept in mint condition. It was never used to lead manure and the wheels never turned on the land except when it was being loaded in a harvest field.

The main purpose for such a vehicle was for transporting goods from the farm to a goods yard and vice-versa. Also, when required, to convey children on their Sunday School outing.

I considered December to be the most miserable I experienced on a horse farm. They were dark gloomy days and adverse weather conditions. Our first day was spent ploughing and we found the ploughs in the same position as they had been left on Martinmas Day.

We never saw the farmstead in daylight, except at noon. It was dark when we left the stable with our pairs of horses and no lamps were carried. It was a ghost procession; the only sound heard was the clip-clop of horses feet. Some mornings, we had 'yoked up' and plough wheels were turning before the dawn. When daylight appeared, the scenery came into view instantly as if by magic. Ploughing continued into the afternoon until the evening shadows began to fall, when once again darkness shrouded the procession homeward bound.

34

On arrival, we watered the horses before entering the stables, where we stripped them of their harness before we had our suppers, so called because it was our last meal. The evening stable work was similar to that which had taken place in the early morning. The horses were fed and groomed, but instead of harnessing them we gave each one a bed of straw. We left the horses warm and comfortable, their bellies full. During our dinner hour at noon, I had refilled the corn bin and the chaff bin. Jim had carried sufficient straw on a fork from the stockyard and stored it in the stable.

The foreman was satisfied if the stubble fields scheduled to grow turnips were ploughed before the end of December. In January it was the turn of the clover fields, referred to a 'Awd Seeds', which had provided pasture for the sheep the previous summer. This was ploughing at its best. The clover roots held the soil together. The straight clean cut furrows and the unbroken ridges the full length of the field created an attractive scene. On a clear dry day, ploughing 'Awd Seeds' on the Wolds with a pair of fine horses was a pleasure.

Farming techniques have completely changed from those far off days and horses are no longer required today. The events which took place at Martinmas are just memories and Pocklington is no longer linked by rail to York. The circumstances concerned with my journey to the farm and the kindness shown to me by a stranger will never be experienced again.

# Early Tram Days in Hull

By A. Mason

It was not long after the Tramways Act of 1870 came into force that a promoter came forward with a scheme to construct a tramway system in Hull. Solicitors representing Major James Holland wrote to the local board of health that their client was proposing to apply to the Board of Trade for a provisional order. In 1871, on November 13th. the application was approved and the tramway committee was set up. Major Holland's scheme was not without controversy. In part of the old town, the streets were only fifteen feet wide (there is a provision in the Tramways Act 1870 to the effect that no rail should be laid nearer to the kerb than nine feet six inches) so, according to that, no track should have been laid in the old town. The original scheme was not only to lay a track, but to lay a double track.

Trinity House, which owned much property in the old town, succeeded in persuading the House of Commons Committee to grant only one line.

Eventually the Hull Tramways Bill came before Parliament, and the Continental and General Tramway Company was authorised to construct the following tramway in Hull.

1. From Suffolk Terrace, Beverley Road to the Crown Inn on Holderness Road. via Beverley Road, Prospect Street, Albion Street, Bond Street, George Street, Charlotte Street, North Street, Bridge Street, over North Bridge and through Witham and along Holderness Road.
2. George Street, joining with tramway number one to Junction Street via Savile Street.
3. Nelson Street to Junction Street via Queen Street; Market Place, Silver Street and Whitefriarsgate. (the old town route)
4. Spring Bank (Derringham Street) to Prospect Street.
5. Anlaby Road (St. Mathews Church) to Wilberforce Monument via Anlaby Road, Midland Street, Osborne Street, Waterhouse Lane and St. John Street.
6. Hessle Road (from the toll bar i.e. Division Road) to Osborne Street joining with number five tramway. via Hessle Road and Porter Street.

The Tramway Committee was dissolved and responsibilities for tramway matters were transferred to the works committee.

After the opening of the first line (the Beverley Road route) The Continental and General Tramway Company was authorised to sell its interest to the Hull Street Tramway Company.

In July, 1873, the Royal Agricultural Show was held in Hull, bringing many visitors from all parts, so if the Anlaby Road line had been in use, it would have been a great advantage to everyone, as the show ground was off Anlaby Road. However, it was not. Instead, work went ahead as planned for the Beverley Road line, which was started in August, 1873, at Suffolk Terrace.

The last horse tram entering Temple Street depot. 1899.

Horse Trams in Savile Street

The works committee kept a keen eye on the work carried out and, not being satisfied at the progress, directed the company to employ a man as overseer and pay him two pounds per week. By June the track had reached Bond Street and in January, 1875, the work was completed. The line was officially opened on Saturday, 9th January.

The first day was a great occasion, 1,116 passengers were carried, there were two trams in use, providing a half hourly service and they were hauled by two Flemish horses. The fare for the whole journey was twopence with a penny fare stage at Beverley Road and Prospect Street corner.

Next followed a period of expansion. The Hessle Road branch opened on the 7th April, 1877. Two trams ran all day providing a twenty minute service.

Anlaby Road line opened shortly after, followed by a line between Spring Bank and the Pier. By 1882 the company owned 121 horses and 25 trams.

Hedon Road was left out of the present planned tramway, so a group of local businessmen got together in 1885 to provide a service which they wanted to carry 'goods and cattle'. After a great deal of opposition it was agreed so, after widening of the many bridges along the road, work began.

They were not going to use horses, but steam locomotion. The first section was ready in May, 1889, from Witham to Lee Smith Street, at a cost of £8,000. It was to go on to Holderness Drain, then the last stage was from there to Marfleet. The engines cost £500 each and there were four of them, the carriages were £240 each, the fare a penny all distances.

In 1896 a whole new system was proposed the electric tram. The Corporation decided to make a public ceremony to mark the laying of the first tram line on the new electric system. In Porter Street on Thursday, the 9th of June, 1898, Alderman Larard, Chairman of the works committee, performed the ceremony.

Both the Hessle Road and Anlaby Road lines were ready and opened on July 5th, 1899. The first electric tram was driven from St. John Street at 3-15pm along Hessle Road to Liverpool Street depot. The streets were decorated and thousands of people lined the route. The Holderness Road section was opened on April 12th, 1900. So began the era of the noisy clanking monster.

When I lived in Perry Street off Anlaby Road, and worked in the town centre, four times a day I boarded the tram. It would come hurtling along from its depot at Wheeler Street, then grind to a halt, sparks shooting out from the wheels, stopping of course, in the middle of the road outside the West Park police box. Up the stairs we would climb to sit on the hard wood polished seats, and away we went, the driver trying to get through the Anlaby Road crossings before they closed for the train.

The stops were then: Bonar Law House, on to Bourne Methodist Chapel, Argyle street. (The motor buses stopped at East Yorkshire garage) next would come West Parade, on to the other side of Park street (opposite the Palace) only stopping to let passengers off, through Carr Lane, stopping at the Maritime Alms Houses corner of Anne Street and so on to the end of the journey to the City Hall. After it had disgorged all the passengers, it went round the City Hall into Waterwork Street to collect those waiting to return with it down Anlaby Road. Stopping at The Regent Cinema, Pease Street, Day Street,

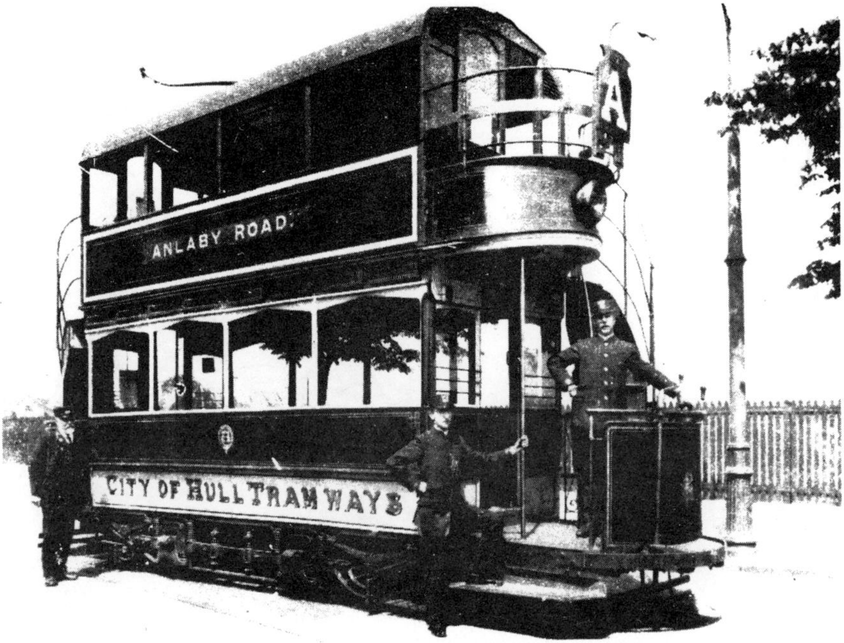

Convent Lane, Linneus Street, Bean Street, Coltman Street. The Boulevard, West Park Cinema, St. George's Road and on to Wheeler Street terminus, where it would go into the shed, turn, and come out again to repeat its journey.

They ran all through the war, come what may, and the conductors always had a joke and a word for everybody. The change over to trolley buses was completed on the 30th June, 1945, when the last tram car (number 169) returned to Liverpool Street depot along Hessle Road, following the same route as the first tram forty six years earlier. As on that occasion, the public turned out in force; an estimated 50,000 people witnessed the last run of a truly remarkable mode of transport.

The Boulevard, Hessle Road.

The Tram Sheds, Holderness Road. 1902-1988.

# Old Bridlington Days

By I. Briggs

I was born in Withernsea in December 1907 and moved with my family to a house in Brooklands Road, Bridlington, in February 1910. One of my earliest Bridlington memories is of being told that the King (Edward 7th) was dead. Then, a little later, of being carried in my father's arms (after normal bedtime) down the full length of St, Johns Street, Quay Road, to the 'Big Lamp' in Prince Street to see the illuminations, celebrating the accession of George 5th. There were no fairy lights or electric signs in those days, but night lights placed in empty glass St, Ivels potted meat jars. Some painted red or blue, interspersed with plain white ones and arranged along the middle sash of the windows. They made good illuminations, or perhaps there was a carriage lamp painted red or blue, containing a burning candle and fixed to the front doors.

A building stood in the middle of the road at the junction of Market Place and High Street Mr Brown's milk business and a chemist's shop. Traffic development caused their demolition. The chemist moved further down High Street and was known as Gatenby's for many years. Also in High Street were Mrs Clarke's shop for ladies' and children's wear. Martindales also sold ladies' wear and there was also Milner's Hardware and iron-mongery with its two bow fronted windows. The grocers, Hutchinson's, was at the corner of Gordon Road and High Street. Doctor Hutchinson lived in the large house which later became a convent school.

At the Westgate end there was 'The Avenue', residence of Mr. Jameson, whose smart carriage drawn by his beautiful high stepping horses, was a well known sight in the town. He had a brother who lived in the end house adjoining the railway line, in the cul-de-sac part of Bessingby Road which faces the side of Bessingby Road bridge. This Mr Jameson could be seen driving his smart trap with his coachman seated beside him. Speaking of carriages, Colonel and Mrs Lloyd Graham of Sewerby Hall drove into Bridlington in their landau which could be seen waiting outside a bank in King Street, or perhaps Richard Allen's fashionable shop on The Promenade, and their coachman with a cockade in his hat seated on the box.

A fashionable wedding took place at the Priory Church when Mr Philip Lloyd Graham, younger son of Sewerby Hall, married the daughter of the Rector of Barmston, a member of the Griffith Boynton family and related to the Cunliffe Lister Family of Masham near Ripon. A little later the bride's aunt left her the Masham estate with the condition that Philip Lloyd Graham took the name of Cunliffe Lister and resided at Masham. He later became Sir Philip Cunliffe Lister and a member of Parliament. Thus it was that, when Colonel and Mrs Lloyd Graham died, Sewerby Hall was sold to Bridlington Corporation because Mr Yarborough Lloyd Graham, the elder son, did not want to live at Sewerby.

Bridlington Corporation invited Amy Johnson to open the newly aquired Hall, her family having associations with Bridlington and, of course, Hull. Amy was accompanied by her husband Jim Mollinson. I was amongst a large crowd that had gathered to hear remarks and admire our famous airwoman.

In the centre of the road at the junction of High Street, St John's Street and Bayle Gate stood the memorial to Alderman John Sawden, later removed to the Priory churchyard because of traffic problems. The grassed area around Bayle Gate was occupied by old cottages, amongst them the ancient Tea Pot Inn, reputed to have smugglers' associations.

Reuben Williamsons horse buses ran from Market Place down to the 'Big Lamp' in Prince Street, the fare all the way was 2d. The bus seats were stuffed with straw and the bus interior was lit by a candle in a carriage lamp. Entrance was by wooden steps up at the back. Sometimes the bus would stop at the corner of Havelock Street for fresh horses to be brought from nearby stables.

People living in the High Street area still called the town 'Burlington' or 'Bollington' and spoke of the Quay area as if it was a separate place. The Workhouse on Marton Road was open, with its inhabitants in their drab clothing. The old National School was replaced by Burlington Elementary School on Marton Road. Moorfield Road School was then Oxford Street School. Moorfield Road was known as Gas House Lane. Other schools were Girls' High School, Boys' Grammar School, Commercial School Trinty Road (boys), Devonshire House School (girls), and West Street Elementary School, Southside.

The Harbour, Bridlington early 1900's

An area which has now gone was Garden Walk and Garden Cottages situated behind Queen Street. The cottages were built facing the harbour with sloping gardens in front. I remember one day idly looking across the harbour, just in time to see one front garden quietly slide down into the harbour mud, and a startled occupant rush to her door and gaze down into the sudden hole in front of her home. Further down Garden Walk was historic Queen Henrietta's House, now sadly demolished. At the end of Queen's Square were the 'baths' where for some years a one armed instructor taught swimming and acted as custodian of the building which was used for public dances. In 1910 there were few buildings on the South-side beyond the Spa and the row of boarding houses now hotels facing the Spa.

Opening of Hildathorpe Road and Springfield Avenue.

There was no sea wall as such between the Spa and Mr. Pitt's privately built wall. His watchman/caretaker/handyman lived in a small bungalow type cottage at one end of Pitt's Wall. Woe betide any small boy who tried to climb up the wall from the beach. or clamber down the grassy bank from above. The watchman could run fast and spank very hard.

During the First World War we moved to the South-side. The south beach was a convenient play area. The mobile bathing huts were an attraction. Mrs Bishop assisted and attended the ladies who came for a dip and also washed out used towels, which were strung in a flapping line from a breakwater to a ring in the concrete. Mr Bishop was in charge of the large Shire horse which patiently plodded into the required depth of water pulling the bathing huts. Ladies in varying degrees of timidity or courage descended the wooden steps to flounder for a few minutes, or occasionally swim daintily for a few strokes, before climbing back up the steps into the hut.

1918 brought a family bereavement and one route to Bridlington Cemetery was via Flamborough Road railway bridge, then left along the public footpath which ran across fields now covered by Queensgate Park, St. Oswald Road and Priory Crescent and passing the bottom of the cemetery, coming out in Bayle Gate at the side of Priory Church. This was reputed to be the old fishermen's track for their donkeys, carrying fish from the beach for the Augustine Monks of the old Monastery (St Mary's Priory). Also beginning at Flamborough Road railway bridge was a rough track running alongside the railway embankment and coming out near the present St. Andrew's Road crossing. Various shacks and pig sties lined the track with an occasional parked gypsy caravan. At the Flamborough Road end was Mr. Turner's Stonemasons and Memorial Yard. Springfield Avenue was a cul-de-sac with Lowson Mill at the Gypsy Race end and still working when it was decided to connect the Avenue with Hilderthorpe Road, covering over the Gypsy Race.

There was an official opening of the new thoroughfare. The Corporation, Mayor, Alderman and Councillors, in their respective robes, processed across the new area.

In the 1920s a pageant was organised to commemorate events in connection with the Augustine Priory. Various organisations dressed to represent particular historical happenings. Adult members of the four church choirs robed as Augustinian Monks (my father amongst them) chanted in harmony as the procession wended its way round the town.

Shortly after the First World War an opening was made in St John's Street as an entrance to the new Queensgate, and the buildings of the first council houses to be let at low rents, primarily to help the many returning ex-servicemen looking for jobs and accommodation.

When the old Victorian Rooms with its turreted tower went up in flames one night, a popular concert venue and pier top landmark vanished. The Royal Princes Parade, the Floral Clock so carefully attended by the council gardeners along with those orchestras and their conductors, Enrico Scoma, Gerchom Parkington, Lioneal Johns, Herman Darewski etc. are just a memory now.

Visit by the Lord Mayor and Sheriff of London to the New Spa 1906.

Julian Kandt's Band, Bridlington Spa Hall 1910.

Princes Parade early 1900's.

# Childhood Days in Burton Agnes

By J. Stephenson

I arrived in Burton Agnes in 1938 at the age of six. My father had got the job as 'engine man' at the newly built pumping station. We had lived in Bridlington up until then where my father worked on the harbour maintaining the engines in the fishermen's boats. One of my earliest memories is of a fisherman knocking at our door one night to ask my father to rectify a fault on the engine of his boat. "Thoo'll eve ti cum tiv'er, Ted, she's crammlin aboot sea like a bug in a tar barrel".

Coming to Burton Agnes was my first real taste of country life. I was to remain there for twenty years, except for a break during the war. The village school was nearly a mile away at the other end of the village. I had to walk there summer and winter as did every other child. Some had to walk much further than I. Mrs Cork was the headmistress, a kindly person as far as I could remember, though as an infant I was in Miss Estill's class. Some lessons would not have found a place in the modern 'National Curriculum'. I remember the 'big lads' being allowed out of school during lesson time to catch rats and mice when they were threshing at the farm across the road. They used to display their 'trophies' along the edge of the road in neat rows; there was practically no traffic there then. There always seemed to be an awful lot of rats and mice to me!

I remember learning to read from a wall chart. This series of pictures with accompanying sentences, told the story of a bearded elderly gentleman called 'Old Lob'. The only picture I remember very clearly showed Old Lob in his gig.

We had two school visits whilst I was there, one was to pick snow drops in Crow Wood just up the hill. The other was to stand outside the Hall to watch the Hunt assemble with Lady Wickham Boynton having her stirrup cup. The walk home from school often took a long time. We used to watch Frank Clark working in the blacksmith's shop. You could get nuts from the walnut trees in 'chapel yard' and there were plenty of conker trees. There was a tailor who lived in one of the cottages I passed on my way home. He would give us bobbins for making tanks with an elastic band, a piece of a candle and a matchstick. In addition there was a newt pond opposite my house in those days. I still like newts, but I remember the big lads warning me not to handle the king newt 'cos they'll sting yer'. They were the great crested newt and it was the silver flash in the tail of the male which was supposed to sting.

Nearly all the fields were pasture and full of mushrooms in season. A lot of them were horse mushrooms as big as a dinner plate, but we ate them.

When I look back and re-live these idyllic activities I feel glad to be as old as I am, I have no envy of present day children who are largely denied these simple pleasures. The newt ponds were filled in years ago, the fields are nearly all arable, the hedges are mostly gone and wandering across fields is confined to sign-posted public footpaths.

Then the war came. My father, as an ex-regular in the RAF, was called up immediately. We went up to the school for our gas-masks. My sister, who was two, had to have a Mickey Mouse gas-mask in which she had to be put, screaming in protest. It was all rather exciting to us infants. We all had to learn to knit! When I had knitted one or two six inch squares to help to make a blanket for the soldiers, I was bitten by the 'knitting bug' quite badly and knitted a little pair of mittens for the new baby born at the Harrisons' Farm halfway down the village. This interest soon palled, however, as so many exciting things were happening! Workmen came to put sand-bags in front of the windows at the pumping station, and we had our own guard against parachutists. Every evening at about six o clock, our guard would come from Bridlington to stop the Germans from taking over the waterworks!

One of these men became a great friend. He was a fisherman I believe, and he showed me his rifle with which to defend us. He even showed me the five bullets he kept in a drawer. He also made me a capacious net for catching newts and sticklebacks.

At school we were told where to go if there was an air-raid. I had to run down the hill, past the pond to the post office, where Mrs. Tommy had an Anderson shelter in her garden. Fortunately, although we had one or two practices, I never had to undertake this marathon in earnest. But we did have an air-raid. The Luftwaffe attacked Driffield aerodrome, but it was on their way home, and they were set upon by our fighters. There was no siren but my mother must have known there was some danger, as she put my sister, the cat and me in the 'glory hole'. I could hear a lot of banging and went outside to view the excitement. At that very moment a German bomber flew over, hotly persued by by one of our planes firing at it. I promptly ran screaming back into the 'glory hole' where my mother dosed me liberally with sal-volatile. However, in their panic to escape, some of the German bombers evidently jettisoned their bombs, one of which, as luck would have it, hit an ammunition dump in a nearby field.

Phoebe Clark, my piano teacher, who lived near the pond in the village, rang my mother up to say it might be as well if I didn't go for my lesson that day as there were bits of shrapnel flying about all over the place.

Then the evacuees came. We had an evacuee teacher, Miss Bickle, who actually came to live in our house with us. She was a jolly girl from Hull. I basked in reflected glory at school but, rather to my annoyance, she didn't treat me any differently from the others in the class. However, she was very kind to me outside school and gave me an old copy of Alice in Wonderland which I read avidly and I learnt to ride a bike when she gave me her old fairy cycle.

In the winter of 1940 we left Burton Agnes and did not return until my father took up his job again after the war. Things in the village began to change after that.

As a child, my sporting activities were limited in success but invariably full of incidents. We all played cricket and the

48

'Nursery Ground' was a strip of rough pasture behind the 'Council ooses' along Station Road. The wicket was always a sticky one, but I suppose the theory was that if you could hit the ball at all as it ricocheted off the mole-hills and tussocks of grass you must have an eagle-eye and the reactions of a mongoose.
There was only one kind of bowling, fast. There was no room here for the sneaky subtlety of off-break or leg-break or googly. If you bowled slowly, the bumps and hollows in the pitch guaranteed the ball would never reach the batsman and it was considered quite acceptable, if any budding Jim Laker tried to bowl slow, for the batsman to wait for the ball to stop and then walk down the pitch and clout it anywhere where there wasn't a fielder. Once, however, 'Snipe' Pickering nearly got a hat-trick by bowling slow full tosses on a June evening with the sun behind him.
The advantage was always with the bowler as no ball was ever straight. Neither bowler, batsman, wicket keeper nor anybody else knew in what direction the ball would go once a delivery had hit the ground. Fortunately we only used a soft ball, except once when someone produced a 'corker' and Tally Wilson bowled one of his fast 'googlies' which cracked Bonnard Pickering on the shin. He was not amused and indicated with some feeling that he would "tek is bat yum" if this ball was used again. Since it was his bat, we decided to revert to the 'tenniser'.
It wasn't just the wicket, we used to give it a good bashing with the bat after a vicious delivery had turned through nearly 90 degrees at head height, but that was really to let off our feelings rather than with any hope of taming it, it was also the rules They were original and strictly enforced, largely by Bonnard, the bat owner.
As I have said, the pitch was narrow, skirted on one side by the 'back-ways' of the council houses. Retrieving a ball from some of these meticulously tended vegetable plots was as fraught with danger as Jason's effort to obtain the Golden Fleece. I soon learned that 'gardeners' were out. Naturally, there weren't many 'gardeners', as any luckless batsman who happened to connect with the ball and edge it over the fence had to fetch it himself.
At the opposite side of the pitch was a hedge which cows grazed behind. It was considered a legitimate shot to belt the ball over the edge and you could run for as long as it took to find it. However, a shot over the edge was always risky as it was quite likely the ball would fall in a cow-pat, and as the bowler had to clean the ball it was decreed that 'coo-clappers' were out.
Of course, we never had an umpire - we were all umpires. Disagreements were common. Should we be unable to reach a consensus, the batsman had to undergo three 'bat-handles'. This bizarre but effective method of deciding a batsman's fate operated as follows: the batsman had to turn the bat upside down, thus holding it by the blade. The bowler bowled three balls and the batsman had to try to keep the ball from hitting the wicket.
As can be seen, our approach to the game was to many rather unsophisticated, but it must be said that quite a few players graduated from this preparatory stage and eventually played for Burton Agnes Firsts, though not me!

The Old Schoolhouse at Burton Agnes.

Burton Agnes Church of St. Martin.
Drawings by Mary Randell.

# Boyhood Memories of Brough

*By Paul Everatt*

I spent my formative years in 1924-31 at Brough where my parents shared a tied cottage. This was Lodge Farm in Skillings Lane, a rambling old property owned by my father's employer, a Mr. A. Massey who ran a small soap factory called Newbright Ltd.

Four times a day I had to trudge a mile to and from the C. of E. school in Elloughton. Bus fares were only available in the worst weather. No school meals in those days when you had to subsist on dripping or pepper-and-salt sandwiches. A miniscule bottle of milk served as a thirst quencher. If placed by the school's gas fire it was almost lukewarm by noon. The cloakrooms had no heat - merely a cold tap and a very chipped basin. Boys and girls had separate tarmac playgrounds, each boasting a row of dry toilets.

Highlight of the week was an afternoon out at the school garden, a half acre patch behind Miss Fulstow's haberdashery. Many lads wore tackety boots and sported close-cropped haircuts. These were achieved by their fathers plonking a basin on their heads, near scalping the thatch and leaving a large frontal tuft.

At that time the village probably consisted of some 500-600 souls, but there was little sense of community although I did join the 1st Elloughton-cum-Brough Boy Scout Troop led by Stanley F. Craggs of the local ship-building family.

The village had just four shops, two pubs, one church and a station. We had to provide our own entertainment. With no one to guide us on conservation we blatantly robbed birds' nests for our collections, or took pheasants' and partridge eggs home for omelettes. Milk was delivered from churns brought to the door by the dairyman in his pony and trap. Mother left the cash and the jug on the doorstep with a glass-beaded piece of muslin atop to keep out the insects.

Brough was a reversal terminus of the local train service through Hessle, Ferriby and Melton, hence the trains were a constant source of inte-rest. The coaches were shunted from the 'Down' platform to the 'Up', with the engine then uncoupled, backing off, side-tracking the coaches and then re-connecting at what had become the front end of the train for the return journey to Hull. The level crossing was a focal point; when the road gates were seen to be closing it became a challenge to scoot across the line on foot through the pedestrian gates before the signalman locked them from his box. The station also boasted a goods yard, sidings, and lastly, a footbridge. The latter gave a sky-lark's view of passing traffic and all enveloping clouds of steam and smoke as an added thrill.

The Ferry Inn, Brough near Hull in 1907.

A fascinating development around 1930 was the introduction, for short-haul journeys, of steam rail-cars all named after earlier stage coaches such as 'Tally-Ho' and 'Rockingham'. Two other events involving rail travel were much anticipated. In the summer a special day trip to the seaside, usually Hornsea or Withersea was arranged by the school. Then, in January, the church choirmaster, Dick Curtis, took us into Hull to see the pantomime followed by a slap up tea, this trip being paid for out of the proceeds of the choir's recent carol singing around the village.

Brough golf course was a magnet on Saturdays and during school holidays. As a caddy you could earn 1/6d (7½p) a round with perhaps an extra 3d (1p) tip if you cleaned your players' clubs properly. In the days before stainless steel it was essential to equip yourself with a small piece of emery cloth for this purpose. In evenings fossicking for lost balls could prove a lucrative side-line. On collecting a dozen you posted them off to a firm specialising in re-paints. Providing that the foundlings weren't too badly hacked the effort was usually rewarded with the return of a postal order for 5/- or 6/- (25p) (30p) Due to my church commitments I was not allowed by my parents to caddy on a Sunday. This was much to my chagrin as the going rate on the Sabbath was 2/6d (25p) a round, big money indeed.

An even harder earned few coppers would be produced from a daily morning paper round (6am). A weekly trip totally 18-20 miles paid one shilling or (5p) and there was no shortage of volunteers.

March 1931. Gander Dower's Blackburn Bluebird being towed through Hull City Centre from Dyce for safe keeping in a garage.

Eric Gander Dower (left) with his Blackburn Bluebird after landing at Dyce in March 1931.

The Blackburn Beverley transport plane.

Blackburns' Aircraft Factory was the largest employer in the East Riding. Strategically sited on the Humber bank the firm specialised in the construction of water-borne aeroplanes. Amongst these were large passenger-carrying flying boats such as the 'Perth', 'Sydney' and 'Iris', the latter for the RAF. Because of its novelty the launch of these 15 to 20 ton leviathans attracted considerable public interest. To get one of these giant machines into the air was a major exercise. After being lifted on to a felt-lines launching cradle the plane had then to be manoeuvred adjacent to the slipway. The only vehicle powerful enough to haul this contraption up and over the river bank and down into the water was a local farmer's steam traction engine, normally used for threshing. Launch and recovery could only be effected about two hours either side of high water whilst all river traffic had to be stopped during landing and take off.

The firm also built a landplane, a single-engine bi-plane trainer, the 'Bluebird'. This was unusual in that pupil and instructor were squeezed side-by-side into one cockpit instead of the more usual tandem arrangements.

In 1930 the airfield (and it was literally a field in those days) was visited by Alan Cobham's Flying Circus which was then barnstorming the country. His exhibition included an autogiro, forerunner of the helicopter a wing-walker and a delayed drop parachutist. He also had a large twin-engine passenger monoplane, 'Youth of Britain', in which the public were invited to take a flip over the local villages at 5/- (25p) a time.

Yes, these were hard times, but we were none the worse for this. At least they taught us the value of money. If living conditions were primitive by today's standards we suffered little and enjoyed a healthy rural life.

A recent nostalgic visit to Brough inevitably showed many changes over the sixty years since I left. It was revealed that Lodge Farm, after serving some time as a fish and chip shop, now houses a video library and a unisex hair salon.

# Filey — Episodes and Anecdotes

By G. E. Hume

Filey is a fascinating little coastal resort situated seven miles south of Scarborough.

My earliest recollections of Filey date back to 1903. I was three years old, and was stung by a bee whilst picking flowers on my way up from the beach.

The town is on the fringe of the Wolds. You have only to travel a mile or two in any direction before you come to the 'up and down' roads so typical of the foothills of the Wolds, and a mere five miles takes you right into Wolds country.

Filey is a mixture of old and new. It is a known fact that the Romans had a camp and watch-tower on 'Carr-Naze', the name of the peninsular which leads to the Brig. 'Carr' comes from the ancient British word 'caer' meaning a camp. The supporting stones for the pillars of the tower can be seen in the grounds of the library in West Avenue.

Viking influence can be seen in Filey by observing the shape of the boats, the 'cobbles', constructed after the pattern of the Viking longships. They are unique to the area, their flat bases being well suited to the long haul over the beach for launching. Mounted on wooden wheels they used to be drawn across the sands by horses, but around 1950 tractors took their place.

The town is virtually cut in two, the old and the modern. In Church Hill there are some interesting examples of eighteenth century houses. One of them bears the date 1705.

St. Oswald's Church, which stands above the Ravine on the north cliff was commenced during the reign of King Stephen, and was finished in the year 1114. There have been additions made since then. Visitors who like old churches will find much to interest them in St. Oswald's.

Around 1700 people came by coach, on horseback, or by private carriage to take waters of the 'spa', which were found on 'Carr-Naze'. There is no trace of this 'spa' today.

Queen Street is one of the oldest streets in Filey. Many of the fishermen still live there. You can see their gear in the back gardens. There is a red lamp at the seaward end of Queen Street. It is there to guide the fishermen home when it is dark. Two of the cottages dating from 1696 have been converted to form a 'Folk Museum'. One of the cottages was a dairy with cows in the back-yard.

The principal coaching inn was Foords, with its doric pillars still standing, and still in daily use as a public house. The main shopping streets in the newer part of the town are Murray Street and Belle Vue Street, with John Street linking the two. Union Street and Hope Street are on a smaller scale. Union Street was named as such because it was the first street to link the old Filey with the new one.

Filey is noted for its wide expanse of golden sands, on which you can walk for miles between Filey and the sheer cliffs of Bempton on the way to Flamborough Head. There are lovely walks along the cliff top both north and south of the town, with miniature golf links on each of the cliffs. The Memorial Gardens with their aviary and fountain and Crescent Gardens with their beautiful flower beds, and the Glen gardens with boating pool and putting green. It is interesting to note that what is now the Glen Gardens was once the property of wealthy landowners. In early Victorian days a beautiful Georgian style mansion was erected by Henry Bentley of Bentley's Yorkshire Breweries. The house was named Ravine Villa. The estate included the ravine which was known as Bentley's Gill. There use to be a footbridge across the stream which led to an underground ice-house. In later years the Villa became the property of Edwin Martin, and the ravine became Martin's Ravine. Subsequently the house fell into disrepair and was taken over by the Filey Council. They tried to maintain it by setting up a snack-bar and letting off rooms for various purposes, but it became too expensive to maintain.

It was demolished during the 1960's and the Glen Gardens cafe took its place. The estate became the Glen Gardens. The original lodge still stands at the west entrance to the gardens and is still occupied.

Facing the Crescent Gardens is the beautiful row of houses and hotels which form the Crescent. Some of the hotels have been altered in recent years into flats or apartments. Thankfully the facade has kept its attractive appearance. One of these buildings used to be The Royal Court Hotel, and it was this hotel that Princess Mary took over as the family's holiday home. Lord Harewood and his younger brother played on Filey sands. The building is now an apartment block known as The Royal Crescent Court.

What is now the Council Offices and Tourist Information centre used to be a Convent, and until the mid-sixties was also a school known as the Convent of the Sacred Heart.

The brig is a long peninsular consisting of calcelarious gritstone. It was probably named 'Bryggja' by the Scandinavians, meaning a landing place or jetty. It is fascinating to study the many rock pools full of marine life. For those who prefer to approach the brig from the beach, there is a more or less defined path, devious at times, which will lead them there. Visitors to the brig must always watch out for the changing tide. It can be quite menacing at times, with people having to be rescued by boat.

My mother and other visitors became stranded and had to be taken off the brig in a cobble. The cobble however got into difficulties and another cobble went out to assist. They transfered to the second cobble. It can be imagined how difficult this must have been in the 1920's when long skirts were the fashion and the sea was choppy.

Returning to the pathway along the top of North Cliff, and past where the tower used to be, one can look down to the left and see flat stretches of rock with several large pools. One of these pools is called 'The Emperor's Pool'. It is said that Emperor Constantine bathed in it.

Again from this promontory, looking down to your right, you will see a zig-zag path, partly earth, partly steps, leading down to the approach of the brig. In sunny weather we have seen parties of nuns sitting on the slopes near this path. They have picnics there. Some of the younger ones take of their

St, Oswald's Parish Church, Filey.

shoes, raise their habits and run up and down like children.
    Until recently nuns used to have holiday hostels in Filey. They came in batches and were lovely people. They didn't question your religion, but always greeted you with a smile. One nun we remember with great affection was very stout and very short and very rosy cheeked. She had wrinkled stockings with spots of grease on her habit. She was a cook in one of the hostels, and was as Irish as Irish could be. We had great difficulty in understanding her at first. We use to tease her and call her 'Miss Ireland' which brought a hearty laugh from her. On a remote part of the beach near Primrose Valley, we often saw nuns paddling in the sea. It was a treat to see them enjoy themselves.
    A well respected old Filonian who has since died related this story to me. It appears that a short time ago when a person died, the coffin of the deceased was placed on a trestle outside the house where he or she had lived. On the day of the funeral the coffin was carried to the church by friends of the deceased, by men if it had been a man, or women if it had been a woman. On this occasion it had been a woman. She had been an exceptionally heavily built person, and her friends found great difficulty in carrying the coffin to the church. The vicar had been waiting for some considerable time at the churchyard gate. He must have thought he had made a mistake in the date or the time. However, the cortege did at last appear, and the coffin was literally dropped at his feet. The spokeswoman for the group said, "Eh, parson, we'se sorry to kip you waiting, but she were that evvy we kep avin to av a rest. Now sum un else ull av to tek ovver".

Fisherman's Cottages, Filey.

Fishing Trips.

# The Story of a Waggoner

## By Bill Thompson

Bill Thompson (seated) with his pal Billy Gilson.

A waggoner's job started at a very early age. We were working on farms from the age of thirteen. It was hard work and a long day as everything that came onto a farm or off, was horse driven.

On the 5th August, 1914, about twelve hundred of the farms got their calling up papers. We had to report to Bradford Moor Barracks that day. There were about thirty who got on the train at Middleton, and one or two had had too much to drink, so the policemen put them on the sweep's handcart, (which I knew very well from my school days,) and put them on the train.

My next move was to Aldershot where we arrived about teatime. After tea three of us went down to town. On the way we met a column of artillery led by an officer on horseback. We did not salute him so he whipped his horse round and gave us a telling off. It was hard to make him understand that we had just joined up and did not know a thing about army rules.

Next day we got a pair of horses and a waggon and while we were waiting to go abroad one or two of us would get jobs collecting blankets. These horses were farm horses and used to blinkers, so when we got on the waggon they bolted and ran into a block of houses where they were drilling fifty or sixty men in the square. The men being drilled ran in all directions. It was all very frightening, but when we got abroad the horses soon tired. They were the same as us, dead tired.

We got to Le Havre by train. They put eight horses in a cattle waggon, four at each end; that left four drivers and a spare man for the centre part.

The civilians loaded us up with apples. At our age we could almost live on them as we were very often hungry.

On the retreat we never knew when or where we were going to get our rations. We landed up at Mons on the Saturday night and pulled into a small field where men were digging latrines. On Sunday morning we were yoking up and making for the gate. That was the start of the retreat from Mons. We were tired out and so were the horses; you could not keep them awake.

Some German cavalry had been seen but they were only scouting and they did not bother us. Our officer had pulled us off the main road. He put three waggons across each end of the column. It was the only time I have heard of men being asked to do anything in the army. Our officer was in tears. I do not know whether he was thinking of us lads having no training or of himself. He asked for anyone who thought they could keep awake to man each end of the waggon column.

When we were on the retreat again, we kept going on as long as horses and men were able to. Tired out we fell asleep whilst driving. Your reins used to fall from your hands. Some lads tied them to the waggon. I kept them in my hands, but I knew where to find them as I was so used to horses. If you had them tied to the waggon and anything happened they could upset the waggon.

When we got going again, we came to some crossroads and we took the correct road. You see we never had any lights. There were times when we pulled into a field after dark and we could not see the waggon lines at all. We slept under our waggons if it was dry, and sometimes the lads would dash under their waggon and find a dead horse there.

There were times when we were lousy; we could not get washed for several days. When it was very hot we would take our shirts off. If we had a few matches or a candle we would run the flame up the seam. The lice use to crack like burning wild oats. They use to sit with their heads to the centre of the seam, massed as thick as a piece of wood. They did not bite me but felt uncomfortable running about.

We were rushed along to cross a certain bridge before it was blown up. It was very tiring for the horses, finishing the retreat some twelve miles from Paris. They pulled us into a field where I have never seen so many dead horses at one time. Our clothes were taken off and put into a large disinfecting machine. When they came out we had a job finding our own clothes.

If you were caught slipping off into the town your were punished by being lashed to the waggon wheels

First time I went up at night, I went through some villages. I was going about a mile and half parallel with the front line. You did not know when was the best time to go as they shelled all such places after dark. We dumped our load in an old ruin whilst bullets were hitting the walls. We had to stand by our horses no matter what was going on.

On the Somme I often met a lot of soldiers coming out of the trenches when I was on a job and should have known a lot of the lads. But for mud and the want of a shave, they were completely unrecognizable. Little did I know that I would be one of them later on.

I often wonder if many people gave a thought for the hundreds of thousands of horses that had to be drafted to horse lines for four and a half years, especially during winter and other bad days. Only half the number of horses were under cover at any one time. They were left out in open fields in all kinds of weather. Every horse had a new rug but it was often under its body. It did not matter how you fastened it, the horses and blankets were covered in mud.

The first time I went into the trenches was with the 1st 19th London Regiment. We had had one month's training at Le Havre and were then sent up the lines.

There were five waggoners and two London lads. We stayed together as long as we could. One of the London lads wanted to look over the top. We begged him not to, but he had his own way and was shot there and then and dropped by my side.

We suffered so many casualties we only stayed the night, and by the following nightfall we were relieved and made our way to the old village for some mud soup as we used to call it. It was so named because when you were walking around, the mud would splash into your mess tin. If the horses came by or a shell fell near by you were covered in mud.

I remember sleeping in an old trench with a bit of old zink on top of me. I was with three or four other lads who I did not know. The next day we were moved to another area and put into a school which was gassed very heavily. We came out of that lot with about a third of our battalion.

The time when I met my pal coming in (Billy Gilson from the Thwing area) I was going out. He had been badly wounded on his head. I handed him over to the first aid post and thought to myself that I would never see him again. After the war I went to Hull fair with my wife and got on a tram on Beverley Road, and to my surprise who was on the tram but my pal Billy and my brother. I did not know they knew each other. He died just five years after the war. He was a brave lad. In the army he was what was known as a runner, taking messages along the lines at all times and in terrible conditions.

My longest night in the trenches was at Armentien. I was due to go on leave the next morning so I was hoping the Germans would keep quiet that night and let me get down the road to a station.

Sometimes we would find a high place where we could go and watch the shelling. You could follow the front line for miles. It was Sunday morning and we were about 200 yards from the German trenches. Our troops were a mixture of regiments. In the area we crossed a very large valley and when we got to the otherside we got in a trench just below the hill top. Coming up behind us was a column of artillery. They came over the first hill and set down in full view of the Germans. They were a sitting target. We got a good view of them being massacred, and I do not think any horses or men got out alive. Had they stayed behind the hill they would have been much safer. There were scores of mistakes made on both sides.

I often sent the walking wounded off if I thought they could make it on their own, because we were very short of men. The only ride we had whilst I was in the infantry was from a place called Cambrai. There were a lot of old London buses, open topped double deckers. But that was the only time we had a ride, otherwise wherever we went we had to walk. The waggoners could do it. They were use to it, as on the farms they had to follow the plough and other implements.

One time when I was coming in from no-man's-land, I was dead tired and worn out. My medical officer could see it and told me to go into the dug out and have a few hours sleep, which I did until the next morning. He then gave me four German prisoners, and I did not like the idea as they could have knocked me out when we had to go into no-man's-land, so I went and got a hand grenade off one of my pals, then I let my prisoners know if they did anything out of the ordinary I would use it.

We went to Abberville and had about three weeks rest. We knew that afterwards we would be going into something pretty big, and it was.

We went back to the Somme area and stayed in a wood for the night. Just before daylight we moved up to the front and laid against some tape which ran for about 100 yards in front of the first trench. We did not know how far the tape ran, whether it was a mile long or not. A barrage started at 4 am.

There were none of us in the front trenches and that was where we got a lot of casualties when they had to pass through the trench as they were a standing target for quite a long time.

That was the first time that I had seen tanks and cavalry in action together. The date was the 24th September, 1918. and it was one of my son's birthdays and his son's birthday. It seemed such a coincidence.

The Germans kept falling back from the 24th September until Armistice day. I went on leave and landed back just three days before the war was over. I did not get back to the front line.

It was on 11th January 1919 before I left for home. I had a month's holiday and got married. It was two years before I got a settled job. I used to say that I would never go back on a farm. Eventually I put in for a foreman's post at Bainton Bank where I stayed for four years before moving on to improve myself and have a better chance for my family.

We had six in the family and they got off to a good start. We went to Mr. Beachill at Holme Wold and stayed there for 18 years before moving to Money Pot Farm in 1943 where we again stayed for many years.

Horses being dispatched to war from Hedon station 1916.

# Chicken Joe and the Shamrocks

By J. W. Stephenson

No, it is not the name of a pop group but, as older readers will recall, these were two of the attractions at Hull's great annual fair in the years between the wars. The fair seems to have been part of the life of Hull for ever, so much so that people would speak of 'Hull Fair Weather' or reckon other events as before or after 'Hull Fair Time'. It brought trade and visitors to the city, of course; people came in from the Wolds and Holderness and the New Holland Ferry brought folk from Lincolnshire anxious to see what Yorkshire had to offer.

Actually it started in the year 1278 when the good monks of Meaux asked their Abbot to petition King Edward 1st for permission to hold a fair at Wyke on Hull. The petition was successful and, although Meaux Abbey is long gone, the monk's excursion into the world of free enterprise is with us to this day.

Wyke grew into the thriving city of Kingston upon Hull and its fair was held annually in late spring. In those distant times it lasted for as long as thirty days; possibly reflecting its importance as a meeting and trading centre serving a wide, though thinly populated, area. In 1598 Queen Elizabeth 1st granted a charter moving the opening date to September and restricting the duration to sixteen days. Still later the opening date of a seven day fair was changed to October 11th. These early fairs were largely concerned with the sale of horses and cattle and the activities of entertainers, pedlars and the sellers of gew-gaws played only a minor role. However, by the late 19th century all live-stock dealing took place at separate events and Hull Fair was entirely given over to providing pleasure and entertainment for the populace.

That part of Hull known as the 'Old Town' was the home of the fair at this time but with the expansion of Hull's dockland in the east, a westward migration down Anlaby Road became necessary in 1865. Corporation Field in Park Street was the first site chosen but the presence of a railway crossing, later replaced by a road bridge, caused problems.

A move to Argyle Street was followed by the final move to Walton Street thirteen years later. This move was expected to cost several hundred pounds and one Councillor suggested that the fair be allowed to die out.

It didn't die out of course and along with fairs at Topcliffe and Boroughbridge remained an important meeting place for many clans of Romany travellers.

In bye-gone days it was also the once-a-year break in the monotonous lives of ordinary folk. Now-a-days the most sophisticated entertainment comes into our homes at the touch of a switch but even in the 1920's it was an important event in Hull. Children in particular endured an agony of anticipation as from early October a trickle, later to become a flood, of showmen began to arrive on the western outskirts of the city. Huge trailers drawn by traction engines bore such names as Bostock and Wombwell or Corrigan and promised the thrills of menagerie or circus. The components of rides and roundabouts could be made out too, the cake walk, the walzers and galloping horses to name but three. As opening day drew nigh the fairground became the scene of feverish activity as its gloomy cinder-surfaced expanse was transformed into a wonderland.

The fair was important enough to warrant an opening ceremony performed by the Lord Mayor of Hull, and on the appointed day he was driven the length of Walton Street to the fair-ground. Here a charter ratified by Edward 1st in 1299 was read out and the fair declared open.

Every day it would come to life around noon but somehow in the afternoon it seemed a little tame, even tawdry. When the cloak of darkness had fallen, then things were different and its special magic enfolded children and adults alike.

For the whole of fair week Walton Street was closed to traffic, allowing the pavements to be filled with booths and small stalls. These provided candy-floss, brandysnap, toffee apples and nougat for those with a sweet tooth. Should you desire something less sweet, other stalls offered roasted chestnuts, cockles and mussels or, since this was Hull, delicious fish and chips wrapped in paper from which the vinegar would drip.

For a more lasting memento there was cheap jewellery, crockery at knock down prices, patent medicines or even a corn cure. Some householders even rented out their downstairs front-rooms to the fair people. Often these were taken by lady palmists or fortune-tellers, remarkable, most claimed allegiance to the Smith or Lee families. At night some stalls were illuminated by electric light but even in the mid 1920's many still had gas or acetylene lanterns. Whatever the source of light the effect was to produce a glowing, golden ribbon of luminosity slicing through the velvety black of night.

You could alight from a crowded tram in Anlaby Road or Spring Bank West and immediately plunge into the heady atmosphere of Walton Street.

The ears were assailed by the cries of stall-holders, the eyes dazzled by a myriad lights and the nostrils titillated by the smell of tasty delicacies. In the press of people progress was slow indeed, no more than a shuffle.

At last the fair ground entrance would be reached and here the glare of lights seemed to turn night into day. High on the sky-line the tall, slim Helter Skelter was picked out in glowing light bulbs. In the background, taller than the other rides, the tassled and netted bulk of the Shamrocks rose and fell rythmically. Those huge, multi-seat swings with squealing young and old were also picked out in light bulbs. The reason for the squeals was not far to seek, for the apex of each swing the car was tilted at such an angle that its brightly decorated underside was revealed.

In the fair-ground proper you became engulfed in sound, invitations to ride on this, enter that, visit the circus or even join in the boxing.

The brassy music of the steam-organs with their tinny percussion filled the air and the whole dizzy confection was enveloped in a faintly sulphurous, though not unpleasant, smell of smoke.

For what is by today's reckoning a trivial sum, you could be whirled around, shaken to and fro, swung back and forth, terrified by a tiger or maybe frightened to death on the ghost train. While you regained your senses you could be thrilled by acrobats, amused by clowns, become the proud possessor of a stuffed rabbit or even win a toothsome fowl at Chicken Joe's stalls. Of course dad had to show his skills by actually knocking down a coconut with a well aimed wooden ball.

Should you venture close to the three fenced sides of the fair-ground there were occasional glimpses of 'behind the scenes'. A gleaming caravan, trim curtains at the windows and the glint of china and brass within. But watch where you are putting your feet: thick, black, rubber-covered cables snake across the ground delivering electric power from generators. These humming machines were driven by great steam engines resplendent with polished brass and brightly painted fly wheels.

Alas, it seems to be the way of all good things that they should come to an end and midnight on the last day saw the lights extinguished and the steam organs fall silent. Next morning, tents, booths and rides were dismantled and made ready to move off. Walton street was open for traffic once more and in a day or two at the most the showmen had departed. Once more the fair ground became silent and deserted, just a cinder covered expanse with only rain filled hollows to reflect the pale gas lights of Walton street.

BIGGER, BRIGHTER & BETTER THAN EVER
CHICKEN JOE
THE MAN YOU ALL KNOW

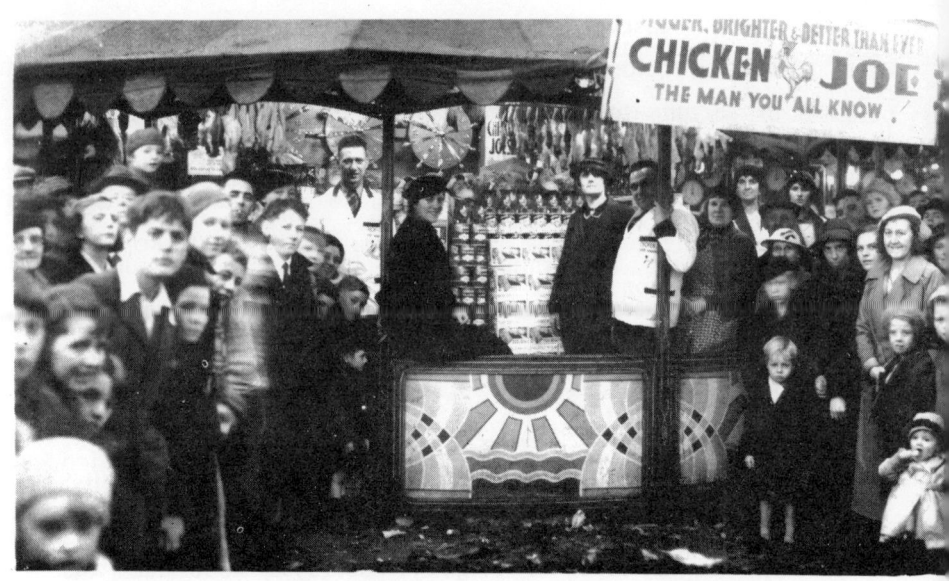

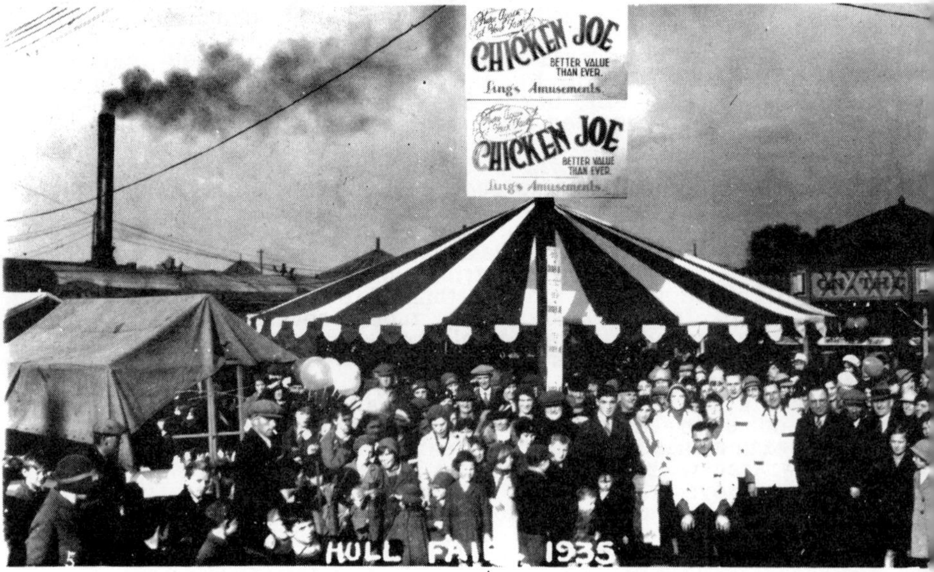
CHICKEN JOE
BETTER VALUE THAN EVER.
Ling's Amusements.
CHICKEN JOE
BETTER VALUE THAN EVER.
Ling's Amusements.
HULL FAIR 1935

# A Train Spotter Remembers
By Mike Wilson

While other young men were mis-spending their youth in the Bash Hall at Bridlington playing snooker, I passed mine lounging on railway stations waiting for a 'cop.'No, not a policeman, but a steam locomotive not seen before.
These locomotives had numbers which were avidly collected and then underlined in blue or red in an Ian Allen Locospotter's Book (He, whoever he was, must have made a small fortune out of us!).
My friends and I spent hours along side the railway line at Bridlington at 'Beezy', so called because it was on the lane to the village of Bessingby. Long lost summer Saturdays and Sundays were spent playing our version of the Test Match, with intermittent breakes when someone shouted 'Pegged In'. This meant that the signal allowing the arrival of another train had changed to green when the semaphore arm dropped, and the cricketers ran to the lineside fence to peer down the line towards Carnaby to be the first to correctly say what type of engine was on its way.
D-49s, Buns (B-1s), B-16s, K-3s and D-20s were common on the Bridlington to Scarborough line, but occasionally the shout "Black Five" or "Jubilee" would go up, denoting that the train was from further afield, usualy somwhere in the West Riding, hauling its hundreds of holidaymakers.
Infrequent visitors were V-2s from York or Doncaster, B-12s from East Anglia, and on a rare occasion an Ivatt C-1 made what was probably one of its last journeys to bring a shout of glee that everyone had 'copped it'.
Tankers, engines with no separate water or coal tender, were sneered upon as having no value, everyone eagerly seeking to add a new 'namer' to their collection. Many locomotives had name plates after antelopes, bearing exotic names like Oryx, Umseke, Impala, Gemsboc and Pronghorn, while others of that class bore the names of top railwaymen of the LNER. D-49s were named after the counties and hunts through which the LNER ran. The first of this class was Yorkshire, with Bedfordshire, Huntingdonshire and Lancashire being 'shedded' either at Hull or Bridlington more or less permanently along with the little 'tankers' for the Malton Dodger duty.
A locomotive was 'shedded' to a locomotive depot, where it was oiled and greased, coaled and watered and, occasionally, cleaned and polished before its crew began their tour of duty up and down the coastal line and back.
Bridlington had a pair of 'coffee pots' shedded there for many years, mainly to do shunting duty in the goods yard, now covered by the new Tescos. These engines were basically a square block box, with four tiny wheels, chain driven by a small steam engine. There was none of the glamour of the larger locos about them, just the matt black of soot and coal dust mixed with the brown of rust and the black paint.

Steam days in Bridlington.

I remember clambering up the station bridge, when it had those iron humps up the middle looking for all the world like the Loch Ness Monster embedded in the tarmac, to see below me a Director class loco on platform five, the departure line for Hull. My box brownie came into action and the result was sent off to a Meccano Magazine photo competition. Sometime later I heard from them with a postal order for half a crown (12½p) as a prize.

The area where Bridlington shed used to be, its code was 53D, a subdivision of Hull (53A), is now covered by B&Q, and the Scarborough side of the station, which used to be platforms one and two, has also disapeared in the cause of progress, New housing now covers the land.

There is now no need for the very long sidings to the south of Bridlington, where, every Saturday during the summer season, strings of carriages of all kinds were shunted to await their hordes of weary holidaymakers later the same day. No longer is there a turntable, on which the locomotives were turned round. Many's the time we've lent a puny arm to turn a visiting Black Five, when we thought we could evade the shed foreman. Many's the time we have gone back home to our long suffering mothers, with our hands, faces, clothes and hankies black with soot after 'cabbing' an enging on shed.

The Multiple-units which ply between Hull and Scarborough through Bridlington are definitely no match for the sight of even a D-49 setting off from Bridlington, wheels slipping, smoke belching black, and steam hissing as the guard flagged it away. Despite 'progress', I doubt if the travellers get to Driffield, Beverley or Hull any quicker or in any more comfort than we did all that time ago.

# Life in Sproatley in the 30's

By *Stanley L. Cooper*

My first view of the village which was to have such a deep influence upon my boyhood was when, on a fine sunny morning in early summer 1925, we moved from Hull to Sproatley. I was three and half years old.

Our new home was the small cottage, now demolished, which squatted between the chapel and the Constable Arms. It overlooked the village green, the scene of many village activities including the fox hunt meetings, horses been broken in, and in the evenings the village youths congregating beneath the large chestnut tree. One notable occasion was when the Blackshirts addressed a crowd on the green, trying to stir up unrest among the farm workers, with little success.

The increase in our family made a move into something larger necessary, and in 1928 we took the tenancy of the last house in Church Lane.

My father came to some arrangement with the previous occupier, a Mr Herdsman, and acquired his muzzle loading shotgun. It was complete with gunpowder, shot, etc. He spent many hours trying to load and fire it without success. One evening however, he casual aimed at a school of crows flying over, pulled the trigger, and hey-presto it fired like a clap of thunder, with a muzzle flash a foot long. He finished up on his backside among the feathers and hen muck. I dont ever remember seeing the gun again, and the event was never ever mentioned within his hearing.

Church Lane is bordered by Horse Chestnut trees which meet overhead, and at that time the rectory, church and school on one side and five cottages on the other. Our neighbour was Mr and Mrs Ball. She ran the small general store in the village (now a chippy) and before marrying Mr Ball was the village cobbler with a room next to her shop.

John Ball was a good story teller with a keen sense of humour. He had a stiff leg, and rode a bicycle so adapted that one pedal remained stationary, whilst he cycled with the other. In the winter he found the best way to keep his stiff leg warm was to wear a lady's stocking on it. He joked that he and his wife could never go out together as they shared the same pair of stockings.

Mrs Ball was a good neighbour and friend. She had black hair and a remarkable peaches and cream complexion. Their life was saddened by the loss of their only child, Cecil, who was drowned in the Humber. She lived to a fine old age of 93. John died some years earlier.

Also in the lane lived the Hobsons, Ograms, and Smiths. Mr Smith had a lorry and was a local carrier.

Living near St. Swithins Church I became a choirboy. The vicar was the Rev, Mr. Dunsby. We had a full choir in those days, and each boy took his turn at pumping the organ.

The school was divided into three classes. Mrs. Thompson taking infants, Mrs. Rhodes juniors and Mr. Thompson, seniors. Mrs. Thompson was a kindly soul who, on the rare visits of the school dentist, had the task of holding our heads still, her face reflecting her concern and horror while the dentist performed. The children then returned to their classes with a bleached face, the bloody tooth as a trophy.

I retain a lasting impression of Mrs. Rhodes, with her hair forming a bun at the back of her head, and a passion for English and poetry. Mr. Thompson was a keen disciplinarian, and was very proficient with the cane. Six of the best and your name in the punishment book was not an unusual event.

Those were the days of the British Empire. The whole school paraded in single file to salute the Union Jack on Empire Day, and Royal Oak Day was the occasion for wearing an oak leaf in your button-hole.

Hardship was widespread during the slump of the thirties and poverty looked in at many cottage windows. I recall Mr. Thompson having set the class to write a composition on 'what I did on Saturday'. One girl wrote that she had bread and maggie-ann for breakfast, and her brother had bread and dip. "What on earth is maggie-ann and dip?" he asked the class. His question was met by the silent puzzled gaze of his pupils - surely everyone knew that!

Our lives as children seemed to follow a well ordered pattern. At Easter, boys got whips and tops and girls skipping ropes. It was also the time for new shoes, if you were lucky. Spring was also the time to visit Primrose Dike and Bluebell Woods. I shall always remember my first visit to Bluebell Woods, where I stood enthralled at the spectacle of a carpet of blue as far as the eye could see, and the total silence except for the sigh of the wind high in the tree canopy. It was like entering a Cathedral.

The pupils of Sproatley school c1930.

In the wetlands near the village were Yellow Flag Irises and Blue 'Milkmaid' flowers; also Watercress and Samphire could be collected. Then and now Easter was a popular time for weddings. I remember a couple marrying at the chapel and leading the wedding procession on foot to the Bride's house for the wedding breakfast. No Bride in a bedecked carriage could look more radiant.

We had six weeks summer holidays and it seemed to last forever. It seldom rained and we used to burst the tar bubbles in the road. In the harvest fields we chased the rabbits who dashed from the slowly reducing area of standing corn in the centre of the field. The farmers wife brought the men's 'llowances to the field, and always seemed to have just enough left over for each lad a piece of pie and half a mug of tea.

I can only recall three people having cars in the village in the early thirties, Mr. Fell the butcher, Mrs. Thompson the school mistress and a young chap who had a win on the Irish Sweepstake. He bought a white S.S. Jaguar (what would that be worth today)?

Before the housing development made it a Dormitory area, the village was small and compact. Even after the lapse of fifty years I can remember it as it was. Starting at the Police Station the village bobby was PC Kilvington. At one end of Tradesmen's Row lived the Riley family. There was the post office with the letter box let into the front of the house. At the other end of the Row lived the blacksmith. I spent many hours watching him shoe the Shire Horses. He also kept cows in the paddock were the row of bungalows now stand. Next came Mr. Fell, the butcher, the Cockerlines and Mrs. Ball's shop. The Constable Arms, our old cottage and the old chapel over looking the green. Down Park Road was the Clares, Miles, and Rileys. Mrs. Riley was a pillar of village life and the one to whom everyone turned for help, be it birth, sickness, death or advice. At the Park Lodge lived the Wilcox family.

Sproatley entertainment, The Fisher Girls 1907.

Returning towards the village and opposite the chapel was Atkinson's farm, now demolished and built over. He was known as Coalie Atkinson, but I only knew him as a farmer, later at West Newton. Our milk lady lived in Cockpit Row, and her greeting was always "Hello you". In a garden at the other end of the row was the cock pit, now built over.

The village institute was a warm haven on a winter's night, and I spent many hours watching the 'big uns' playing snooker, and listening to the dry, pithy humour so typical of the countryman.

Lound's Grocery shop, later with post office, was followed by Harrisons who had a joinery business as well as the village petrol pumps. On the side of the hill was Robinson's farm, now the entrance to a development of bungalows. And finally the Blue Bell Inn.

I shed no tears at leaving school at fourteen. There was no work locally and eventually I got a start at the Cod Liver Oil Factory at Marfleet. A long ride of nearly ten miles each way. In the summer the pilots of the Tiger Moth aeroplanes at Hedon aerodrome would 'buzz' us by swooping down low over our heads as we cycled by, along Staithes Road. I wonder how many of them became members of the 'few' who saved this country from invasion in the last war.

The distance to work and the need to find jobs for a growing family presented a problem and in 1938 we moved back to Hull. After the war I married and returned to the country at Keyingham where my two daughters were brought up. In the fullness of time they too have taken obvious delight in revisiting the lanes and byways of their childhood. And I relived once more the salad days of my boyhood, when life was the speed of a horse, doors were never locked, churches were an ever open sanctuary of peace, and the arrival of valium and vandalism was still fifty years away.